PHP 8 for Web Development

Build Robust, Dynamic Websites with PHP 8 and MySQL

Greyson Chesterfield

COPYRIGHT

DISCLAIMER

The information provided in this book is for general informational purposes only. All content in this book reflects the author's views and is based on their research, knowledge, and experiences. The author and publisher make no representations or warranties of any kind concerning the completeness, accuracy, reliability, suitability, or availability of the information contained herein.

This book is not intended to be a substitute for professional advice, diagnosis, or treatment. Readers should seek professional advice for any specific concerns or conditions. The author and publisher disclaim any liability or responsibility for any direct, indirect, incidental, or consequential loss or damage arising from the use of the information contained in this book.

Contents

Chapter 1: Getting Started with PHP 8 and MySQL

Introduction to PHP and MySQL

PHP and MySQL are two foundational technologies in web development, responsible for powering millions of websites worldwide. PHP (Hypertext Preprocessor) is a server-side scripting language designed primarily for web development but also used as a general-purpose language. MySQL is an open-source relational database management system widely used in web applications to manage data, store user information, and provide dynamic content.

A Brief History of PHP and MySQL

PHP was initially created in 1994 by Rasmus Lerdorf to track visits to his online resume. What began as a simple project evolved into a powerful tool for developing dynamic web pages. Over the years, PHP gained popularity due to its ease of use and flexibility, forming the backbone of many popular content management systems (CMSs) such as WordPress, Joomla, and Drupal.

MySQL was created around the same time, by a Swedish company called MySQL AB. It quickly became popular due to its open-source nature, stability, and efficiency. Together, PHP and MySQL form the "LAMP" stack (Linux, Apache, MySQL, PHP) that has served as a trusted framework for web development for decades. Today, PHP 8 introduces a new era for PHP by improving performance and adding modern features such as Just-In-Time (JIT) compilation, union types, named arguments, and more.

Why PHP 8?

PHP 8 has introduced several performance and usability improvements, making it even better suited for building fast, dynamic websites. Key features include:

1. **Just-In-Time (JIT) Compilation**: JIT allows PHP code to be compiled into machine code at runtime, significantly improving performance for resource-intensive operations.

2. **Union Types**: Union types allow variables to accept multiple data types, which adds flexibility in complex applications.

3. **Named Arguments**: PHP 8 introduces named arguments, enabling developers to specify arguments by their names, which increases readability and reduces errors.

4. **Error Handling Improvements**: PHP 8 introduces a more robust error handling model with enhanced exceptions, making debugging easier.

5. **Null-Safe Operator**: This new operator simplifies null checks, which helps reduce code verbosity.

Together, these features make PHP 8 an even more powerful choice for modern web development. Paired with MySQL, PHP 8 allows developers to build dynamic, data-driven web applications more efficiently than ever before.

Setting Up Your Development Environment

To start developing with PHP 8 and MySQL, you need a local development environment. This environment allows you to write and test code locally before deploying it to a live server. Here's a step-by-step guide on setting up PHP 8, MySQL, and a web server on various operating systems.

Step 1: Install PHP 8

For Windows

1. **Download PHP**: Visit the official PHP website and download the latest stable version of PHP for Windows.

2. **Extract PHP**: Extract the downloaded file to a directory on your system, for example, C:\php.

3. **Add PHP to the PATH**: To use PHP from the command line, add C:\php to your system's PATH variable:

   o Open System Properties > Advanced System Settings > Environment Variables.

   o In the System Variables section, find the Path variable, click Edit, and add the path to PHP.

4. **Verify Installation**: Open Command Prompt and type php -v. If installed correctly, this command should display the PHP version.

For macOS

1. **Install Homebrew** (if not already installed): Open Terminal and enter:

bash

```
/bin/bash -c "$(curl -fsSL
https://raw.githubusercontent.com/Homebrew/install/
master/install.sh)"
```

2. **Install PHP**: Once Homebrew is installed, install PHP by running:

bash

```
brew install php
```

3. **Verify Installation**: Run php -v in Terminal to confirm PHP installation.

For Linux

1. **Update Package Manager**: Open Terminal and update your package manager:

bash

```
sudo apt update
```

2. **Install PHP 8**: Install PHP by running:

bash

```
sudo apt install php
```

3. **Verify Installation**: Check the installation by running php -v.

Step 2: Install MySQL

MySQL can also be installed locally to create, manage, and interact with databases.

Windows

1. **Download MySQL**: Visit MySQL's official website and download the MySQL Installer for Windows.

2. **Run the Installer**: Open the installer and select the "Server Only" installation type.

3. **Set Up MySQL Root Password**: During setup, you'll be prompted to set a root password. Remember this, as it will be used to access the database.

4. **Verify Installation**: Open MySQL Workbench or use the command prompt to log in by running:

bash

mysql -u root -p

macOS and Linux

1. **Install via Homebrew (macOS)** or apt (Linux): Run the following commands:

bash

brew install mysql   # macOS

```
sudo apt install mysql-server   # Linux
```

2. **Start MySQL Service**:

   o   macOS: brew services start mysql

   o   Linux: sudo service mysql start

3. **Set Root Password**:

   o   On first login, run sudo
       mysql_secure_installation and follow the
       prompts to secure MySQL.

Step 3: Set Up a Local Server (XAMPP or MAMP)

XAMPP (Windows, macOS, Linux)

1. **Download XAMPP**: Visit XAMPP's official
   website and download the latest version.

2. **Install XAMPP**: Follow the installation
   prompts to complete setup.

3. **Start Services**: Open XAMPP Control Panel
   and start the Apache and MySQL services.

4. **Test PHP Installation**: Open a browser, type
   http://localhost, and XAMPP's dashboard
   should display, indicating that the local server is
   running.

Hello World with PHP

With PHP and MySQL installed, let's create a simple
PHP script to verify that PHP is working correctly.

Step 1: Create Your First PHP Script

1. **Open Your Text Editor**: Open a text editor like VS Code, Sublime Text, or Notepad++.

2. **Create a New File**: Save a new file named index.php in your web server's root directory. In XAMPP, this is usually C:\xampp\htdocs on Windows and /Applications/XAMPP/htdocs on macOS.

3. **Write Hello World Script**:

php

```php
<?php
echo "Hello, World!";
?>
```

4. **Save the File**: Make sure to save index.php in the correct folder so that your server can access it.

Step 2: Run the Script

1. **Open Your Browser**: Type http://localhost/index.php into the address bar.

2. **View the Output**: If everything is set up correctly, you should see Hello, World! displayed on the screen.

This simple exercise verifies that PHP is properly installed and that your server is running correctly.

Conclusion

In this chapter, you've learned about the background of PHP and MySQL and how these two technologies have become a cornerstone of web development. With PHP 8's new features, web development has become more powerful and efficient, making it easier to build complex applications. You've also set up your development environment, installed PHP, MySQL, and a local server, and ran your first PHP script, "Hello World."

This foundational setup is critical as you continue through the book and build more complex applications. With your local development environment in place, you're now ready to dive into PHP's syntax, control structures, and functions, which we'll cover in the next chapter.

Chapter 2: PHP Fundamentals

Now that you've set up your PHP development environment, it's time to dive into the language itself. This chapter covers the fundamentals of PHP, from basic syntax and variables to control flow and functions. Mastering these core concepts will provide you with the building blocks to create complex, dynamic web applications.

Basic Syntax and Structure

PHP is a server-side scripting language that executes on the server and sends HTML to the client's browser. Let's start with the essentials of PHP syntax and explore variables, data types, and operators.

Writing PHP Code

PHP code is written within <?php and ?> tags. For instance:

php

```
<?php
echo "Hello, World!";
```

?>

Everything outside of these tags is treated as plain HTML, allowing you to seamlessly integrate PHP with HTML on web pages.

Variables

Variables in PHP store data that can be manipulated throughout your script. A variable name in PHP begins with a dollar sign ($), followed by the variable name:

php

```php
<?php
$name = "Alice";
$age = 30;
?>
```

In this example, $name stores the string "Alice", and $age holds the integer 30.

Variable Naming Rules:

- Must start with a $ sign.
- Can contain letters, numbers, and underscores, but cannot start with a number.
- PHP variables are case-sensitive, so $Name and $name are considered different variables.

Data Types

PHP supports several data types:

1. **String**: Text enclosed in quotes.

```php
$message = "Hello, PHP!";
```

2. **Integer**: Whole numbers, positive or negative.

```php
$number = 42;
```

3. **Float**: Decimal numbers.

```php
$price = 19.99;
```

4. **Boolean**: Represents true or false.

```php
$is_logged_in = true;
```

5. **Array**: A collection of values.

```php
$colors = ["red", "blue", "green"];
```

6. **Object**: An instance of a class (explored further in later chapters).

7. **NULL**: A variable with no value.

php

$value = NULL;

Operators

Operators are used to perform operations on variables and values:

1. **Arithmetic Operators**: Perform basic mathematical operations.

php

```php
$sum = 10 + 20;   // Addition
$product = 5 * 6;  // Multiplication
```

2. **Assignment Operators**: Assign values to variables.

php

```php
$a = 10;
$a += 5; // Equivalent to $a = $a + 5;
```

3. **Comparison Operators**: Compare values.

php

```php
$result = (10 > 5); // true
```

4. **Logical Operators**: Used in conditional statements.

php

```php
$loggedIn = true;
$hasPermission = false;
$access = $loggedIn && $hasPermission; // false
```

Control Flow

Control flow structures allow you to dictate the flow of the program based on conditions. PHP's main control flow structures are if statements, switch statements, and loops.

If-Else Statements

The if statement executes code only if a specific condition is true. Adding else and elseif allows you to specify additional conditions.

php

```php
<?php
$age = 20;
```

```php
if ($age >= 18) {

    echo "You are an adult.";

} else {

    echo "You are a minor.";

}
?>
```

In this example, the message "You are an adult." displays if $age is 18 or older. Otherwise, "You are a minor." appears.

Switch Statements

The switch statement allows you to compare a variable against multiple possible values, making it useful for handling multiple conditions.

php

```php
<?php
$day = "Tuesday";


switch ($day) {
    case "Monday":
        echo "Start of the week!";
        break;
```

```php
    case "Tuesday":
        echo "It's Tuesday!";
        break;
    default:
        echo "It's just another day.";
        break;
}
?>
```

In this example, the script will output "It's Tuesday!" because $day matches "Tuesday".

Loops

Loops allow you to execute code repeatedly until a condition is met. PHP offers several types of loops:

1. **While Loop**: Runs as long as a condition is true.

php

```php
<?php
$counter = 0;
while ($counter < 5) {
    echo "Count: $counter <br>";
    $counter++;
```

```
}
?>
```

2. **For Loop**: Commonly used when you know the exact number of iterations.

php

```php
<?php
for ($i = 0; $i < 5; $i++) {
    echo "Iteration: $i <br>";
}
?>
```

3. **Foreach Loop**: Used for iterating over arrays.

php

```php
<?php
$colors = ["red", "blue", "green"];
foreach ($colors as $color) {
    echo "Color: $color <br>";
}
?>
```

Working with Functions

Functions allow you to organize and reuse code, making programs modular and easier to debug. Let's look at the basics of defining and calling functions in PHP.

Basic Function Syntax

To define a function, use the function keyword, followed by the function name and parentheses.

php

```php
<?php
function greet() {
    echo "Hello, World!";
}
greet();
?>
```

In this example, calling greet() displays "Hello, World!".

Function Parameters and Return Values

Functions can accept parameters to work with variable inputs and can return values.

php

```php
<?php
```

```php
function add($a, $b) {

    return $a + $b;

}


echo add(5, 3); // Outputs 8

?>
```

The add() function accepts two parameters and returns their sum.

PHP 8 Named Arguments

PHP 8 introduced **named arguments**, which allow you to specify arguments by their names when calling a function, improving readability:

php

```php
<?php
function greet($firstName, $lastName) {

    echo "Hello, $firstName $lastName!";

}


greet(lastName: "Doe", firstName: "John"); // Outputs "Hello, John Doe!"

?>
```

This approach can be especially useful when functions have multiple optional parameters.

Union Types in PHP 8

With **union types**, PHP 8 allows a parameter or return value to accept more than one data type. This feature is especially useful for flexible functions that handle various types of input.

php

```php
<?php
function displayNumber(int|float $number) {
    echo "The number is: $number";
}


displayNumber(42);     // Outputs "The number is: 42"
displayNumber(3.14);   // Outputs "The number is: 3.14"

?>
```

In this example, the displayNumber function accepts both integers and floats, increasing its flexibility.

Variable Scope

Variables within functions are **local** by default, meaning they are not accessible outside the function.

To access a variable from outside a function, you can use the global keyword or pass it as a parameter.

php

```php
<?php
$name = "Alice";

function greet() {
    global $name;
    echo "Hello, $name!";
}

greet(); // Outputs "Hello, Alice!"
?>
```

While global can be useful, it's generally better practice to pass variables as parameters to avoid unintended side effects.

Anonymous Functions and Closures

PHP supports **anonymous functions** (functions without a name), which can be useful for callbacks or one-time use functions:

php

```php
<?php
$greet = function($name) {
    return "Hello, $name!";
};


echo $greet("Alice"); // Outputs "Hello, Alice!"
?>
```

You can also use closures to capture variables from the surrounding context.

Conclusion

In this chapter, we explored the fundamentals of PHP syntax and structure, covering essential concepts such as variables, data types, and operators. We also learned about control flow structures (if, switch, and loops), which dictate the flow of a program based on conditions. Finally, we introduced functions in PHP, including parameter handling, return values, and PHP 8's new features like named arguments and union types.

Mastering these basics provides a solid foundation for building more complex, dynamic applications in PHP.

As you move on to the next chapter, keep practicing with small scripts to reinforce these core concepts. Each exercise will help you become more comfortable with PHP syntax and programming logic, setting the stage for more advanced topics.

Chapter 3: Object-Oriented Programming in PHP

Object-Oriented Programming (OOP) is a programming paradigm that uses "objects" to model real-world entities. By organizing code into reusable classes, OOP enables developers to write more modular, maintainable applications. In this chapter, we'll explore the core concepts of OOP in PHP, covering classes, objects, inheritance, interfaces, traits, polymorphism, and finally, namespaces and Composer for efficient code management.

Introduction to OOP

OOP provides a structured approach to programming by using classes to define the properties and behaviors of real-world objects. This approach simplifies complex systems by breaking them down into individual components.

Classes and Objects

In PHP, a **class** is a blueprint that defines properties (attributes) and methods (functions) for an object. An **object** is an instance of a class, representing a specific entity with data and behaviors defined by its class.

Defining a Class

Here's a simple class example:

php

```php
<?php
class Car {
    public $make;
    public $model;

    public function startEngine() {
        return "Engine started";
    }
}
?>
```

In this example, Car is a class with two properties, $make and $model, and a method startEngine().

Creating an Object

To create an instance of a class, use the new keyword:

php

```php
<?php
$myCar = new Car();
$myCar->make = "Toyota";
$myCar->model = "Corolla";
echo $myCar->startEngine(); // Outputs "Engine started"
?>
```

Here, $myCar is an object of the Car class. We've assigned values to its properties and called its method.

Constructors

A constructor is a special method automatically invoked when an object is created. In PHP, constructors are defined with __construct().

php

```php
<?php
class Car {
    public $make;
    public $model;
```

```php
    public function __construct($make, $model) {

        $this->make = $make;

        $this->model = $model;

    }


    public function startEngine() {

        return "Engine of $this->make $this->model
started";

    }

}


$myCar = new Car("Toyota", "Corolla");

echo $myCar->startEngine(); // Outputs "Engine of
Toyota Corolla started"

?>
```

The constructor initializes the object with $make and $model when it's created.

Inheritance

Inheritance allows a class to inherit properties and methods from another class, promoting code reuse and reducing redundancy. In PHP, the extends keyword indicates that one class inherits from another.

php

```php
<?php
class Vehicle {
    public $type;

    public function honk() {
        return "Beep!";
    }
}

class Car extends Vehicle {
    public $make;
    public $model;
}

$car = new Car();
echo $car->honk(); // Outputs "Beep!"
?>
```

In this example, Car inherits the honk() method from the Vehicle class.

Advanced OOP Concepts

Once you understand basic OOP principles, advanced concepts like interfaces, traits, and polymorphism will help you write more flexible and powerful code.

Interfaces

An **interface** defines a contract that any implementing class must follow. It specifies methods without providing their implementations, allowing different classes to implement the same interface in different ways.

php

```php
<?php
interface Drivable {
    public function drive();
}


class Car implements Drivable {
    public function drive() {
        return "Driving a car!";
    }
}
```

```php
class Bike implements Drivable {

    public function drive() {

        return "Riding a bike!";

    }

}


$car = new Car();

echo $car->drive(); // Outputs "Driving a car!"

?>
```

Both Car and Bike classes implement the Drivable interface, each providing its version of the drive() method. Interfaces promote consistent behavior across different classes.

Traits

Traits allow classes to reuse methods from multiple sources, solving the problem of single inheritance (i.e., a class can only inherit from one other class). Traits are a way to "mix in" methods from various sources into a class.

php


```php
<?php
```

```php
trait Electric {

    public function charge() {

        return "Charging battery";

    }

}


trait Fuel {

    public function refuel() {

        return "Refueling";

    }

}


class HybridCar {

    use Electric, Fuel;

}


$car = new HybridCar();

echo $car->charge();  // Outputs "Charging battery"

echo $car->refuel();  // Outputs "Refueling"

?>
```

In this example, HybridCar can use methods from both Electric and Fuel traits.

Polymorphism

Polymorphism allows objects of different classes to be treated as objects of a common superclass or interface. This enables you to write code that works with objects of various types in a unified way.

For example, using the Drivable interface from earlier, we can demonstrate polymorphism:

php

```php
<?php
function startDriving(Drivable $vehicle) {
    return $vehicle->drive();
}


$car = new Car();
$bike = new Bike();


echo startDriving($car); // Outputs "Driving a car!"
echo startDriving($bike); // Outputs "Riding a bike!"
?>
```

Here, startDriving() accepts any object that implements the Drivable interface, demonstrating polymorphism by treating Car and Bike uniformly.

Namespaces and Composer

As projects grow, managing code and dependencies becomes challenging. PHP provides **namespaces** and **Composer** to help organize and manage code effectively.

Namespaces

Namespaces allow you to group related classes, functions, and constants, reducing the chance of name conflicts in larger projects. Define a namespace at the beginning of a file:

php

```php
<?php
namespace Vehicles;

class Car {
    public function startEngine() {
        return "Engine started";
    }
```

```
}
?>
```

To use this class in another file, include the namespace:

php

```php
<?php
require 'Car.php';

use Vehicles\Car;

$myCar = new Car();
echo $myCar->startEngine(); // Outputs "Engine started"
?>
```

Namespaces help structure code by logically grouping related classes, improving readability and maintainability.

Composer

Composer is a dependency manager for PHP that automates the process of installing, updating, and managing libraries and packages. Composer helps keep dependencies consistent across development environments and streamlines project setup.

Setting Up Composer

1. **Install Composer**: Visit Composer's official website and follow installation instructions for your operating system.

2. **Initialize a Project**: Navigate to your project's root directory and run:

bash

```
composer init
```

3. **Adding Dependencies**: To add a package, use composer require, for example:

bash

```
composer require monolog/monolog
```

This command installs the **Monolog** library (a popular logging tool) and creates a vendor directory containing the package.

Using Autoloading

Composer provides an **autoloading** feature to load classes automatically, eliminating the need for multiple require statements.

php

```php
<?php
require 'vendor/autoload.php';

use Monolog\Logger;
use Monolog\Handler\StreamHandler;

$log = new Logger('myLogger');
$log->pushHandler(new StreamHandler('app.log',
Logger::WARNING));

$log->warning('This is a warning message');
?>
```

Composer simplifies dependency management and ensures all required libraries are available without manually loading each one.

Conclusion

In this chapter, we explored Object-Oriented Programming (OOP) in PHP, starting with foundational concepts like classes, objects, and inheritance, then progressing to advanced topics such as interfaces, traits, and polymorphism. OOP principles allow you to organize code efficiently, making it modular, reusable, and easier to maintain. Finally, we covered namespaces and Composer, tools that enhance code organization and simplify dependency management.

Understanding and applying OOP will enable you to build sophisticated, scalable applications in PHP. By the end of this chapter, you should feel comfortable with OOP basics and ready to start integrating these concepts into your own projects. The next chapter will focus on interacting with databases in PHP, further enabling dynamic web applications.

Chapter 4: Advanced PHP 8 Features

PHP 8 introduces several powerful features designed to improve performance, readability, and error handling in applications. In this chapter, we'll explore some of the most impactful new features in PHP 8, including JIT compilation, attributes, match expressions, and the null-safe operator. We'll also look at structured error and exception handling, followed by practical use cases showing how these features can be applied in real-world web development.

New PHP 8 Syntax

The PHP 8 update brings fresh syntax that enables more efficient coding and boosts application performance. Let's dive into four key new syntax features: JIT compilation, attributes, match expressions, and the null-safe operator.

Just-In-Time (JIT) Compilation

One of the most significant changes in PHP 8 is the introduction of the Just-In-Time (JIT) compiler, which can compile portions of PHP code into machine code at runtime. This is particularly beneficial for applications that require high computational performance, as JIT can improve speed, especially in

CPU-intensive tasks like image processing, complex calculations, and scientific computations.

How to Enable JIT

JIT is part of the Opcache extension in PHP. To enable it, update the php.ini configuration file:

ini

```
opcache.enable=1

opcache.jit_buffer_size=100M

opcache.jit=tracing
```

With these settings, JIT compilation will be activated, and you should notice performance improvements in CPU-bound tasks.

Use Cases for JIT

For general web applications, JIT may offer minor performance improvements; however, JIT's real impact is on tasks requiring intensive computation. Examples include:

- **Real-time data processing**: Applications that analyze large datasets in real-time.

- **Image processing**: Generating complex graphics or editing high-resolution images.

- **Scientific calculations**: Running simulations or processing large sets of data, like weather forecasting.

Attributes

Attributes, also known as annotations in other languages, allow you to add metadata directly to classes, functions, methods, and properties. This metadata can be used by the PHP engine or third-party libraries to dynamically alter application behavior.

Attributes are declared using the #[AttributeName] syntax.

php

```php
<?php
#[Attribute]
class Route {
    public function __construct(
        public string $path,
        public string $method = 'GET'
    ) {}
}


#[Route(path: "/home", method: "GET")]
```

```
function homePage() {

    echo "Welcome to the homepage!";

}
?>
```

In this example, the Route attribute adds metadata to the homePage function, allowing it to be identified as a route for the /home URL. This technique is often used in frameworks for routing, dependency injection, and validation.

Use Cases for Attributes

Attributes are beneficial when working with frameworks or custom libraries that need to add metadata to various parts of the code. Practical uses include:

- **Routing**: Annotating methods to define URL endpoints.

- **Dependency Injection**: Marking classes or functions that need dependencies.

- **Validation**: Specifying validation rules directly on properties or parameters.

Match Expressions

The match expression is a new, concise way to handle multiple conditional branches, providing a more readable alternative to lengthy switch statements. Unlike switch, match evaluates and returns a value, does not require break statements, and can perform strict comparisons.

php

```php
<?php
$status = 404;

$message = match ($status) {
    200 => 'OK',
    404 => 'Not Found',
    500 => 'Internal Server Error',
    default => 'Unknown Status',
};

echo $message; // Outputs "Not Found"
?>
```

In this example, match checks $status and returns a corresponding message. match expressions are especially useful for cases with multiple conditions, where it's necessary to evaluate and return a result.

Use Cases for Match Expressions

- **HTTP Status Codes**: Simplifying responses based on HTTP status codes.

- **Error Messages**: Returning specific error messages or handling different types of exceptions.

- **Data Transformation**: Mapping input values to different outputs without verbose if or switch statements.

Null-Safe Operator

PHP 8 introduces the null-safe operator ?->, which simplifies checking if an object or property is null before accessing its value. This operator short-circuits if any part of the chain is null, avoiding errors from attempting to access properties or methods on a null value.

php

```php
<?php
$user = null;


// Without null-safe operator
if ($user !== null && $user->profile !== null) {
    $avatar = $user->profile->avatar;
}
```

```
// With null-safe operator

$avatar = $user?->profile?->avatar;
```

In this example, the null-safe operator simplifies the syntax by handling the null checks inline. If $user or $user->profile is null, $avatar is automatically set to null.

Use Cases for the Null-Safe Operator

- **Optional Relationships**: Accessing properties of an object that may not exist, such as an optional user profile.

- **Nested Data**: Simplifying null checks in deeply nested objects or arrays.

- **Conditional Data Access**: Streamlining data access in cases where some elements may be undefined or null.

Error Handling in PHP 8

PHP 8 refines error handling, making it more robust and introducing more detailed error messages. Structured exception handling in PHP 8 helps developers catch and handle exceptions more effectively.

Custom Exceptions

Creating custom exceptions allows for more specific error handling. By extending the Exception class, you can define unique error messages and codes.

php

```php
<?php
class CustomException extends Exception {}

function divide($a, $b) {
    if ($b == 0) {
        throw new CustomException("Division by zero is not allowed.");
    }
    return $a / $b;
}

try {
    echo divide(10, 0);
} catch (CustomException $e) {
    echo "Error: " . $e->getMessage();
}
?>
```

In this example, CustomException is thrown when attempting to divide by zero, and it is caught in the catch block, which displays an error message.

Enhanced Error Messages

PHP 8 provides improved error messages, helping developers identify issues more accurately. Errors now include detailed information on function calls, file paths, and line numbers.

Example of Enhanced Error Message

Consider the following example:

php

```php
<?php
function test($value) {
    return $value->property;
}


test(null);
?>
```

In PHP 8, this will throw a clear error message indicating that an attempt was made to access a property on a null value, helping developers locate and resolve issues faster.

Exception Chaining

PHP 8 supports **exception chaining**, where a new exception can be thrown in response to a previous one, preserving context. This helps when debugging complex code flows by providing more information about the error's origin.

php

```php
<?php
try {
    try {
        throw new Exception("Initial error");
    } catch (Exception $e) {
        throw new CustomException("Secondary error", 0, $e);
    }
} catch (CustomException $e) {
    echo "Error: " . $e->getMessage() . " Previous: " . $e->getPrevious()->getMessage();
}
?>
```

Here, CustomException is thrown in response to an initial Exception, allowing both errors to be displayed and traced.

Practical Use Cases

Now let's look at some practical examples of where these features optimize real-world applications in PHP 8.

Case Study 1: Dynamic Data Processing with JIT

For an e-commerce platform that calculates shipping costs based on location, weight, and volume, using JIT can significantly speed up calculations, especially when applied to high-traffic systems or global shipping platforms.

php

```php
<?php
function calculateShipping($distance, $weight) {
    return $distance * 0.5 + $weight * 0.3;
}
```

echo calculateShipping(200, 20); // Outputs a calculated shipping cost

With JIT enabled, this calculation is faster, especially beneficial when repeated for multiple items or orders.

Case Study 2: Simplifying Routing with Attributes

Frameworks can benefit from attributes to define routes for each page, reducing the need for manual configuration. Here's an example of defining a route for a blog application:

php

```php
<?php
#[Route(path: "/post/{id}", method: "GET")]
function showPost($id) {
    return "Displaying post with ID: $id";
}
?>
```

With attributes, each route is defined directly on the function, streamlining routing and improving readability.

Case Study 3: Null-Safe Operator in User Profiles

A social media application may display a user's profile picture, but not all users have uploaded one. With the null-safe operator, displaying an avatar becomes simpler:

php

```php
<?php
$user = getUser();

$avatar = $user?->profile?->avatar ?? 'default.png';
echo $avatar; // Outputs either the avatar path or 'default.png' if no avatar is set
?>
```

Conclusion

In this chapter, we explored some of PHP 8's most powerful new features. The Just-In-Time compiler brings performance enhancements, particularly beneficial for computationally intensive tasks. Attributes offer a new way to add metadata, streamlining processes like routing and validation. The match expression simplifies conditional logic, while the null-safe operator enhances data handling by reducing null checks. Additionally, improved error handling and structured exception management provide clearer and more specific error messages.

Together, these features empower PHP developers to write more efficient, readable, and maintainable code, allowing you to build faster and more reliable web applications. As you continue working with PHP 8, these tools will help you streamline development and optimize performance.

Chapter 5: Introduction to MySQL and Database Basics

Databases are central to most web applications, providing a way to store, retrieve, and manage data efficiently. MySQL is a popular open-source relational database management system (RDBMS) widely used for building dynamic, data-driven applications. In this chapter, we'll cover the basics of MySQL, including setting up MySQL, creating databases, understanding SQL commands, and performing CRUD (Create, Read, Update, Delete) operations. We'll also explore how to connect PHP to MySQL, enabling interaction between your application and the database.

MySQL Basics

Setting Up MySQL

Before working with MySQL, you need to install it on your local environment. If you're using a package like XAMPP or MAMP, MySQL may already be installed as part of the bundle. To confirm, open your terminal or command prompt and type:

bash

```
mysql -u root -p
```

If MySQL is installed, this command should prompt you for a password. Enter the root password you set during installation.

Starting MySQL Service

For users on Linux or macOS, you may need to start the MySQL service manually:

- **macOS**: Run brew services start mysql (if installed via Homebrew).

- **Linux**: Run sudo service mysql start.

Once MySQL is running, you're ready to start creating databases and tables.

Creating a Database

A **database** is a collection of data organized into tables, each with rows and columns. To create a database, log into MySQL and run the following command:

sql

```
CREATE DATABASE my_app;
```

Here, my_app is the name of the database. You can verify that it was created by running:

sql

```sql
SHOW DATABASES;
```

To start working within this database, use the USE command:

sql

```sql
USE my_app;
```

Understanding Basic SQL Commands

Structured Query Language (SQL) is the language used to interact with databases. Let's explore some essential SQL commands.

Creating a Table

To store data, you need to create a table within your database. A **table** consists of rows and columns, where each column represents a specific data type (e.g., text, integer, date). Here's an example of creating a users table:

sql

```sql
CREATE TABLE users (
    id INT AUTO_INCREMENT PRIMARY KEY,
    name VARCHAR(50),
```

    email VARCHAR(100),

    age INT

);

In this example:

- id is an integer that auto-increments with each new user, making it a unique identifier.

- name and email are VARCHAR fields for storing text up to a specified length.

- age is an integer.

Inserting Data

To add data to a table, use the INSERT command:

sql

INSERT INTO users (name, email, age) VALUES ('Alice', 'alice@example.com', 25);

This command inserts a new row into the users table with a name, email, and age.

Retrieving Data

To retrieve data, use the SELECT command. The following query retrieves all rows and columns from the users table:

sql

```sql
SELECT * FROM users;
```

To retrieve specific columns, specify them in the query:

sql

```sql
SELECT name, email FROM users;
```

Updating Data

To modify existing data, use the UPDATE command. Here's how to update Alice's age:

sql

```sql
UPDATE users SET age = 26 WHERE name = 'Alice';
```

The WHERE clause ensures that only the record matching name = 'Alice' is updated.

Deleting Data

To delete data from a table, use the DELETE command. Here's how to remove Alice's record:

sql

DELETE FROM users WHERE name = 'Alice';

Again, the WHERE clause is essential to prevent deleting all records.

CRUD Operations

CRUD (Create, Read, Update, Delete) operations are fundamental to database management. Let's go through these operations in more depth using real-world examples with the users table.

Create

The INSERT statement allows you to create new records in a table. Here's an example:

sql

```
INSERT INTO users (name, email, age) VALUES ('Bob', 'bob@example.com', 30);
```

After executing this command, a new user record is created with the specified details.

Read

The SELECT statement retrieves data from the database. You can filter data using conditions. For example, to find all users older than 25:

sql

```
SELECT * FROM users WHERE age > 25;
```

Sorting and limiting results is also possible. For instance, to get the top 5 oldest users:

sql

```
SELECT * FROM users ORDER BY age DESC
LIMIT 5;
```

Update

The UPDATE statement modifies existing records. Here's how to update a user's email address:

sql

```
UPDATE users SET email = 'bob.new@example.com'
WHERE name = 'Bob';
```

This command changes Bob's email address to the new one.

Delete

The DELETE statement removes records from the table. For example, to delete all users under 18:

sql

```
DELETE FROM users WHERE age < 18;
```

The WHERE clause here is crucial; without it, all rows in the users table would be deleted.

PHP and MySQL Integration

To create dynamic applications, you often need to connect your PHP scripts to a MySQL database. PHP provides various ways to connect to MySQL, with PDO (PHP Data Objects) being a popular and secure choice for database interaction.

Connecting to MySQL Using PDO

The following code snippet demonstrates how to connect to MySQL using PDO:

php

```php
<?php
$host = 'localhost';
$db = 'my_app';
$user = 'root';
$pass = 'password';


try {
    $pdo = new PDO("mysql:host=$host;dbname=$db", $user, $pass);
```

```php
$pdo->setAttribute(PDO::ATTR_ERRMODE,
PDO::ERRMODE_EXCEPTION);

    echo "Connected successfully";
} catch (PDOException $e) {

    echo "Connection failed: " . $e->getMessage();

}
?>
```

In this example:

- $host, $db, $user, and $pass define the database connection details.

- The PDO object attempts to connect to the MySQL server.

- setAttribute configures error reporting, making it easier to debug connection issues.

Executing CRUD Operations in PHP

With the PDO connection established, you can now perform CRUD operations directly from PHP.

Create (Insert)

To insert data, use the prepare and execute methods. This example inserts a new user into the users table:

php

```php
<?php
```

```php
$sql = "INSERT INTO users (name, email, age) VALUES (:name, :email, :age)";

$stmt = $pdo->prepare($sql);

$stmt->execute(['name' => 'Charlie', 'email' => 'charlie@example.com', 'age' => 22]);

echo "New user added";

?>
```

Here, placeholders (e.g., :name) prevent SQL injection, a common security vulnerability.

Read (Select)

To retrieve data, use prepare, execute, and fetchAll:

php

```php
<?php
$sql = "SELECT * FROM users WHERE age > :age";

$stmt = $pdo->prepare($sql);

$stmt->execute(['age' => 20]);

$users = $stmt->fetchAll(PDO::FETCH_ASSOC);

foreach ($users as $user) {
    echo $user['name'] . " - " . $user['email'] . "<br>";
}
```

?>

This code retrieves all users older than 20 and displays their names and email addresses.

Update

Updating data with PHP and PDO follows a similar approach. Here's how to update a user's age:

php

```php
<?php
$sql = "UPDATE users SET age = :age WHERE name = :name";
$stmt = $pdo->prepare($sql);
$stmt->execute(['age' => 32, 'name' => 'Bob']);
echo "User updated";
?>
```

In this example, Bob's age is updated to 32.

Delete

To delete a record, use DELETE with prepare and execute:

php

```php
<?php
```

```php
$sql = "DELETE FROM users WHERE name =
:name";

$stmt = $pdo->prepare($sql);

$stmt->execute(['name' => 'Charlie']);

echo "User deleted";

?>
```

This command removes the user with the specified name from the database.

Practical Use Case: User Management System

To bring these concepts together, let's outline a basic user management system. In this system:

1. **Users are stored** in the users table with attributes like name, email, and age.

2. **CRUD operations** allow administrators to create, view, update, and delete users.

3. **PHP scripts** handle the logic, with forms to capture user input.

Creating the User Form

Create an HTML form to capture user details, such as name, email, and age:

html

```html
<form action="create_user.php" method="post">

    <input type="text" name="name"
placeholder="Name">

    <input type="email" name="email"
placeholder="Email">

    <input type="number" name="age"
placeholder="Age">

    <button type="submit">Add User</button>
</form>
```

Handling Form Submission in PHP

In create_user.php, capture the form data and insert it into the database:

php

```php
<?php
require 'db.php'; // Connection file


$name = $_POST['name'];

$email = $_POST['email'];

$age = $_POST['age'];
```

```php
$sql = "INSERT INTO users (name, email, age)
VALUES (:name, :email, :age)";

$stmt = $pdo->prepare($sql);

$stmt->execute(['name' => $name, 'email' => $email,
'age' => $age]);


echo "User added successfully!";

?>
```

This approach allows you to extend the user management system to include features like displaying, updating, and deleting users.

Conclusion

In this chapter, we explored the fundamentals of MySQL and its integration with PHP. We covered essential SQL commands, performed CRUD operations, and learned how to connect PHP to a MySQL database using PDO. With this foundation, you now have the skills to interact with databases, store and retrieve data, and create dynamic applications. This chapter provides the groundwork for building more complex, data-driven PHP applications, which we'll explore further in the next chapters.

Chapter 6: Building Dynamic Web Pages

In this chapter, we'll explore techniques for creating dynamic web pages using PHP. Dynamic content loading allows a page to adapt based on user interactions or data from a database, providing a personalized experience. We'll also discuss how to standardize layouts with reusable templates and learn how to integrate PHP with HTML to handle forms and navigation. By the end of this chapter, you'll have a strong foundation in building user-friendly, dynamic pages with PHP.

Dynamic Content Loading

Dynamic content loading refers to generating page content based on user actions or data stored in a database. Instead of static HTML, which displays the same content to all users, dynamic content changes based on variables like user preferences, database entries, or session data.

Example 1: Displaying User Profiles

Suppose you're building a website where each user has a unique profile page. With PHP, you can create a single profile.php template that loads each user's information dynamically from a database. Here's how to do it.

1. **Retrieve the User ID** from the URL. For example, profile.php?id=3 would indicate a user ID of 3.

2. **Query the Database** for the user's information.

3. **Display the Information** on the profile page.

php

```php
<?php
// Database connection
require 'db.php';

// Retrieve user ID from URL
$user_id = $_GET['id'];

// Fetch user details from database
$sql = "SELECT * FROM users WHERE id = :id";
$stmt = $pdo->prepare($sql);
$stmt->execute(['id' => $user_id]);
$user = $stmt->fetch();
```

```php
if ($user) {

    echo "<h1>{$user['name']}</h1>";

    echo "<p>Email: {$user['email']}</p>";

    echo "<p>Age: {$user['age']}</p>";

} else {

    echo "User not found.";

}

?>
```

In this example:

- $_GET['id'] retrieves the user ID from the URL.

- The database query fetches the user's data, which is then displayed on the page. If the user is not found, an error message appears.

This approach enables each user to have a personalized profile page without creating multiple HTML files.

Example 2: Displaying Content Based on User Role

Let's say your website has different content for regular users and administrators. You can use dynamic content loading to display specific options based on the user's role:

php

```php
<?php
// Assume $user_role is retrieved from session data or database
$user_role = 'admin';


if ($user_role === 'admin') {
    echo "<a href='admin_dashboard.php'>Admin Dashboard</a>";
    echo "<a href='manage_users.php'>Manage Users</a>";
} else {
    echo "<a href='user_profile.php'>View Profile</a>";
}
?>
```

In this example, administrators see links to the dashboard and user management, while regular users only see their profile link. This technique is especially useful for creating role-based access controls on your website.

Using Templates

Templates allow you to reuse the same layout across multiple pages, improving consistency and reducing the need for duplicate code. By organizing code into templates, you can make updates in one place and have them automatically applied across all pages that use the template.

Creating a Basic Template

A typical template might include shared elements like a header, footer, and navigation menu. Let's create a basic template in template.php that includes a header and footer:

php

```
<!-- template.php -->
<!DOCTYPE html>
<html lang="en">
<head>
    <meta charset="UTF-8">
    <title>My Website</title>
    <link rel="stylesheet" href="styles.css">
</head>
<body>
```

```html
<header>
    <h1>My Website</h1>
    <nav>
        <a href="index.php">Home</a>
        <a href="about.php">About</a>
        <a href="contact.php">Contact</a>
    </nav>
</header>

<main>
    <!-- Dynamic content goes here -->
    <?php include($content); ?>
</main>

<footer>
    <p>&copy; 2023 My Website</p>
</footer>
</body>
</html>
```

In this template:

- The header includes the site title and navigation links.

- <?php include($content); ?> dynamically includes the page content, which will be set in each individual page file.

Using the Template in Pages

To use the template in different pages, set $content to the path of the specific page content, and then include template.php. Here's an example for home.php:

php

```php
<?php

$content = 'home_content.php';

include 'template.php';

?>
```

The home_content.php file contains only the unique content for the home page. When home.php is loaded, template.php will render the entire layout, inserting home_content.php in the main section.

Benefits of Templates

Templates make it easy to maintain a consistent layout across your site. For example:

- Updating navigation in template.php automatically reflects across all pages.

- Adding new pages only requires creating a small content file rather than rewriting the entire page structure.

PHP and HTML Interactions

Integrating PHP with HTML allows you to create interactive pages, handle form submissions, and navigate users through various sections of your site. Let's look at practical examples of PHP-HTML interactions.

Example 1: Handling Forms with PHP

Forms allow users to submit data, such as filling out contact information or updating profiles. PHP handles this data on the server side.

Contact Form

Let's create a simple contact form in contact.php:

html

```
<form action="submit_contact.php" method="post">

    <label for="name">Name:</label>

    <input type="text" id="name" name="name" required>


    <label for="email">Email:</label>
```

```html
<input type="email" id="email" name="email" required>

<label for="message">Message:</label>

<textarea id="message" name="message" required></textarea>

<button type="submit">Send Message</button>
</form>
```

When the form is submitted, the data is sent to submit_contact.php using the POST method.

Handling Form Data in PHP

In submit_contact.php, you can use PHP to handle the form submission, validate the data, and send an email or save the message to a database.

php

```php
<?php
// Retrieve and sanitize form data
$name = htmlspecialchars($_POST['name']);

$email = htmlspecialchars($_POST['email']);

$message = htmlspecialchars($_POST['message']);
```

```php
// Perform simple validation

if (!empty($name) && !empty($email) &&
!empty($message)) {

    echo "Thank you, $name! We have received your
message.";

    // Further processing, such as saving to the database
or sending an email, goes here

} else {

    echo "All fields are required.";

}
?>
```

In this example:

- htmlspecialchars() sanitizes user input to prevent cross-site scripting (XSS).

- Basic validation checks ensure that all fields are filled out before processing.

Example 2: Dynamic Navigation

You can use PHP to create navigation menus that change based on the current page or user status.

php

```php
<?php
```

```php
$pages = [
    'Home' => 'index.php',
    'About' => 'about.php',
    'Contact' => 'contact.php'
];


echo "<nav>";
foreach ($pages as $title => $url) {
    $activeClass = ($_SERVER['PHP_SELF'] == "/$url") ? 'class="active"' : '';
    echo "<a href='$url' $activeClass>$title</a>";
}
echo "</nav>";
?>
```

In this example:

- The navigation links are stored in an array.
- Each link checks if it matches the current page and, if so, applies an "active" class for styling.

Combining Templates, Dynamic Content, and PHP Interactions

Let's put everything together by creating a dynamic product catalog page. This page will:

1. **Load product data from a database**.

2. **Display products** in a standard layout using templates.

3. **Include filters or search options** to customize the displayed content.

Step 1: Database Setup

Create a products table in your database with the following structure:

sql

```sql
CREATE TABLE products (
    id INT AUTO_INCREMENT PRIMARY KEY,
    name VARCHAR(100),
    description TEXT,
    price DECIMAL(10, 2)
);
```

Step 2: Fetch and Display Products

In catalog.php, fetch the product data from the database and display it.

php

```php
<?php
require 'db.php';

$sql = "SELECT * FROM products";
$stmt = $pdo->query($sql);
$products = $stmt->fetchAll();

$content = 'catalog_content.php';
include 'template.php';
?>
```

In catalog_content.php, loop through the $products array to display each product:

php

```php
<!-- catalog_content.php -->
<h2>Product Catalog</h2>
```

```php
<?php foreach ($products as $product): ?>

    <div class="product">

        <h3><?php echo
htmlspecialchars($product['name']); ?></h3>

        <p><?php echo
htmlspecialchars($product['description']); ?></p>

        <p>Price: $<?php echo
htmlspecialchars($product['price']); ?></p>

    </div>

<?php endforeach; ?>
```

Each product is displayed within a standard layout, and by modifying the catalog_content.php file, you can customize the catalog's appearance.

Conclusion

In this chapter, we covered essential techniques for building dynamic web pages in PHP. Dynamic content loading enables you to personalize pages based on user data or database content. Templates allow you to reuse layouts, ensuring consistency and reducing code repetition. Finally, we explored practical PHP-HTML interactions, demonstrating how to handle forms and create dynamic navigation.

These skills are fundamental for building interactive, user-centered web applications. As you continue building your PHP projects, keep experimenting with these techniques to create engaging and efficient pages for users. In the next chapter, we'll delve into user authentication and session management, allowing you to create secure, personalized experiences.

Chapter 7: Forms and User Input Handling

Forms are essential for user interaction in web applications, allowing users to submit data that can be processed on the server. However, handling forms requires attention to data validation and sanitization to ensure security and usability. In this chapter, we'll cover the basics of creating and styling forms, techniques for validating and sanitizing input, and advanced methods for handling multiple inputs, file uploads, and date selections.

Form Basics

Creating HTML Forms

HTML forms enable users to input and submit data to the server. Let's create a simple form for user registration.

html

```
<form action="process_registration.php" method="post">

  <label for="name">Name:</label>
```

```html
<input type="text" id="name" name="name" required>

  <label for="email">Email:</label>

  <input type="email" id="email" name="email" required>

  <label for="password">Password:</label>

  <input type="password" id="password" name="password" required>

  <button type="submit">Register</button>
</form>
```

In this example:

- action specifies the PHP file (process_registration.php) that will process the form data.

- method="post" sends the data securely to the server.

- Form fields include name, email, and password, each with the required attribute, ensuring users complete the form before submission.

Styling the Form

Forms can be styled using CSS to enhance user experience and visual appeal. Here's an example of basic styling:

css

```css
form {
    max-width: 400px;
    margin: auto;
    padding: 20px;
    border: 1px solid #ccc;
    border-radius: 8px;
}

label, input {
    display: block;
    width: 100%;
    margin-bottom: 10px;
}

button {
    background-color: #4CAF50;
```

```css
  color: white;

  padding: 10px 15px;

  border: none;

  border-radius: 5px;

  cursor: pointer;

}
```

This styling centers the form, adds padding, and styles the button, making the form easier to use and visually consistent.

Processing Form Data in PHP

When the form is submitted, the data is sent to process_registration.php, where PHP processes it.

php

```php
<?php
// Retrieve form data

$name = $_POST['name'];

$email = $_POST['email'];

$password = $_POST['password'];


// Check if fields are empty (simple validation)
```

```php
if (empty($name) || empty($email) ||
empty($password)) {

    echo "All fields are required!";

} else {

    echo "Registration successful for $name with email
$email.";

}

?>
```

In this example, the script retrieves data from $_POST
and performs a basic validation check to ensure no
fields are left empty.

Validation and Sanitization

Handling form data securely is essential, as improper
handling can lead to security vulnerabilities such as
SQL injection, cross-site scripting (XSS), and data
tampering. Validation and sanitization are key steps in
ensuring data integrity and security.

Validation

Validation checks whether input data meets specific
requirements, such as length, format, or data type. PHP
offers built-in functions to help with validation.

Example: Validating an Email Address

PHP provides the filter_var function, which can validate email addresses:

php

```php
<?php
$email = $_POST['email'];
if (filter_var($email, FILTER_VALIDATE_EMAIL))
{
    echo "Valid email address!";
} else {
    echo "Invalid email address!";
}
?>
```

In this example, FILTER_VALIDATE_EMAIL checks if the input is in a valid email format, helping prevent incorrect or malicious email inputs.

Example: Checking String Length

To ensure a password meets minimum length requirements:

php

```php
<?php
$password = $_POST['password'];
if (strlen($password) >= 8) {

    echo "Password is strong enough!";
} else {

    echo "Password must be at least 8 characters long!";

}
?>
```

This validation checks if the password is at least 8 characters long, a common requirement for secure passwords.

Sanitization

Sanitization removes unwanted characters or formats input to make it safe. This step is crucial for preventing injection attacks or other malicious data manipulation.

Example: Sanitizing Text Input

The htmlspecialchars function is commonly used to sanitize text input, converting special characters into HTML entities to prevent XSS attacks.

php

```php
<?php
$name = htmlspecialchars($_POST['name']);
```

```php
echo "Welcome, $name!";

?>
```

In this example, any HTML tags or special characters in the $name variable are converted, ensuring the text is safe to display on the webpage.

Example: Sanitizing Email Input

filter_var can also be used for sanitizing email addresses:

php

```php
<?php

$email = filter_var($_POST['email'],
FILTER_SANITIZE_EMAIL);

echo "Sanitized email: $email";

?>
```

This removes unwanted characters from the email address, ensuring only valid characters are included.

Preventing SQL Injection

SQL injection occurs when malicious SQL code is inserted into a query, potentially allowing attackers to access or manipulate the database. To prevent this, always use **prepared statements** when working with databases.

php

```php
<?php
require 'db.php';

$name = $_POST['name'];
$email = $_POST['email'];
$password = $_POST['password'];

$sql = "INSERT INTO users (name, email, password)
VALUES (:name, :email, :password)";
$stmt = $pdo->prepare($sql);
$stmt->execute(['name' => $name, 'email' => $email,
'password' => password_hash($password,
PASSWORD_DEFAULT)]);
echo "User registered successfully!";
?>
```

In this example:

- prepare and execute prevent SQL injection by binding parameters safely.

- password_hash adds another layer of security by hashing the password before storing it.

Advanced Input Handling

Beyond basic text fields, forms often include multiple inputs, file uploads, and date selections. PHP provides tools to handle these scenarios efficiently.

Handling Multiple Inputs

Sometimes, a form may include dynamic input fields that allow users to add multiple entries. For instance, if users can add multiple phone numbers, PHP can process each entry as an array.

Example: Handling Multiple Phone Numbers

html

```html
<form action="process_phones.php" method="post">
    <label for="phone1">Phone 1:</label>
    <input type="text" name="phones[]" id="phone1">

    <label for="phone2">Phone 2:</label>
    <input type="text" name="phones[]" id="phone2">

    <button type="submit">Submit</button>
</form>
```

In process_phones.php:

php

```php
<?php
$phones = $_POST['phones'];

foreach ($phones as $phone) {
    echo "Phone number: " . htmlspecialchars($phone) . "<br>";
}
?>
```

The phones[] input name creates an array of phone numbers. The script loops through the array to process each number individually.

File Uploads

PHP supports file uploads, allowing users to submit images, documents, or other files. Handling file uploads requires specific form attributes and validation to ensure files are safe.

Example: Basic File Upload Form

html

```html
<form action="upload_file.php" method="post" enctype="multipart/form-data">
```

```html
<label for="file">Choose a file:</label>
<input type="file" id="file" name="file" required>
<button type="submit">Upload</button>
</form>
```

In this form:

- enctype="multipart/form-data" specifies that the form handles file data.
- The file input uses name="file" for easy access in PHP.

Processing File Uploads in PHP

The upload_file.php script can handle file validation and saving:

php

```php
<?php
if (isset($_FILES['file'])) {
    $file = $_FILES['file'];


    // Validate file type and size
    $allowed_types = ['image/jpeg', 'image/png', 'application/pdf'];
```

```php
    if (in_array($file['type'], $allowed_types) &&
$file['size'] <= 2000000) {

        $upload_dir = 'uploads/';

        $file_path = $upload_dir .
basename($file['name']);


        if (move_uploaded_file($file['tmp_name'],
$file_path)) {

            echo "File uploaded successfully: " .
htmlspecialchars($file['name']);
        } else {

            echo "Error uploading file.";

        }
    } else {

        echo "Invalid file type or file too large.";

    }
}
?>
```

In this example:

- Allowed file types and sizes are checked.

- move_uploaded_file moves the file from a temporary directory to the specified upload location.

- Uploaded file information is sanitized and displayed.

Handling Date Selections

Date fields often require validation to ensure that dates are in the correct format. HTML5 provides a date input type, making date selection easier and more consistent across browsers.

Example: Using a Date Input

html

```html
<form action="process_date.php" method="post">
    <label for="date">Select a date:</label>
    <input type="date" id="date" name="date" required>
    <button type="submit">Submit</button>
</form>
```

In process_date.php, validate the date:

php

```php
<?php
$date = $_POST['date'];
$date_timestamp = strtotime($date);
```

```php
// Check if the date is valid and in the future
if ($date_timestamp && $date_timestamp > time()) {
    echo "Date is valid and in the future.";
} else {
    echo "Please select a future date.";
}
?>
```

The strtotime function converts the date into a timestamp, allowing you to perform date comparisons and validations.

Conclusion

In this chapter, we covered essential aspects of form creation and user input handling in PHP. You learned how to build, style, and process forms, validate and sanitize user data, and handle advanced inputs like multiple fields, file uploads, and date selections. These techniques provide a secure, user-friendly experience and form the foundation for building reliable, interactive applications.

With a strong grasp of form handling and validation, you're now ready to apply these skills to user registration, data entry, and other interactive elements in your applications. In the next chapter, we'll focus on user authentication and session management, allowing you to create secure, personalized experiences for your users.

Chapter 8: User Authentication and Session Management

Authentication and session management are essential components of secure web applications, allowing users to register, log in, and access restricted areas of a site. In this chapter, we'll cover how to build a user authentication system, manage secure sessions, and control access based on user roles and permissions. By the end of this chapter, you'll have the tools to create secure, user-specific experiences in your PHP applications.

Building Authentication

User authentication allows users to register accounts, log in, and manage their passwords. Let's start by building a registration and login system and implementing secure password management.

User Registration

User registration typically involves collecting basic user information (like username, email, and password), validating it, and storing it securely in a database. Let's create a register.php form and a process_registration.php script to handle registration.

Creating the Registration Form

html

```
<form action="process_registration.php"
method="post">

    <label for="username">Username:</label>

    <input type="text" id="username"
name="username" required>


    <label for="email">Email:</label>

    <input type="email" id="email" name="email"
required>


    <label for="password">Password:</label>

    <input type="password" id="password"
name="password" required>


    <button type="submit">Register</button>
</form>
```

Processing the Registration in PHP

In process_registration.php, we'll validate the form data, hash the password for security, and store the user information in the database.

php

```php
<?php
require 'db.php';

$username = $_POST['username'];
$email = $_POST['email'];
$password = $_POST['password'];

// Basic validation
if (empty($username) || empty($email) ||
empty($password)) {
    die("All fields are required.");
}

// Hash the password before storing
$hashed_password = password_hash($password,
PASSWORD_DEFAULT);

// Insert user into the database
$sql = "INSERT INTO users (username, email,
password) VALUES (:username, :email, :password)";
```

```php
$stmt = $pdo->prepare($sql);

$stmt->execute([

    'username' => $username,

    'email' => $email,

    'password' => $hashed_password

]);


echo "Registration successful!";

?>
```

In this script:

- password_hash securely hashes the password using PHP's PASSWORD_DEFAULT algorithm.

- The user information is stored in the database, but only the hashed password is saved, making it unreadable even if the database is compromised.

User Login

The login process involves verifying that a user's credentials match what's stored in the database. Let's create a login.php form and a process_login.php script to handle login.

Creating the Login Form

html

```html
<form action="process_login.php" method="post">
    <label for="username">Username:</label>
    <input type="text" id="username" name="username" required>

    <label for="password">Password:</label>
    <input type="password" id="password" name="password" required>

    <button type="submit">Login</button>
</form>
```

Processing the Login in PHP

In process_login.php, we'll verify the user's credentials, starting by retrieving the hashed password from the database and then using password_verify to compare it with the entered password.

php

```php
<?php
```

```php
require 'db.php';
session_start();

$username = $_POST['username'];
$password = $_POST['password'];

// Retrieve the user by username
$sql = "SELECT * FROM users WHERE username = :username";
$stmt = $pdo->prepare($sql);
$stmt->execute(['username' => $username]);
$user = $stmt->fetch();

if ($user && password_verify($password, $user['password'])) {
    // Set session variables
    $_SESSION['user_id'] = $user['id'];
    $_SESSION['username'] = $user['username'];
    echo "Login successful!";
} else {
    echo "Invalid username or password.";
```

```
}
?>
```

In this example:

- password_verify securely compares the entered password with the hashed password.

- If the credentials match, session variables are set to identify the user, enabling secure access to their data across pages.

Password Management

Implementing secure password management includes allowing users to reset or update their passwords. PHP's password_hash and password_verify functions ensure passwords are stored securely, making it harder for attackers to compromise accounts.

1. **Password Reset**: Send a unique link to the user's registered email to reset their password.

2. **Update Password**: Verify the current password and then hash the new password before storing it.

Using secure methods for password storage and verification is crucial in ensuring account security.

Session Management

Sessions are essential for managing user data during their visit to your application. PHP's $_SESSION superglobal allows you to store information about the user across multiple pages. Proper session management ensures that this data is secure.

Starting and Configuring Sessions

To use sessions, call session_start() at the beginning of each script that accesses session data.

php

```php
<?php
session_start();
$_SESSION['user_id'] = 1;
echo "User ID: " . $_SESSION['user_id'];
?>
```

Once set, $_SESSION['user_id'] is available across pages. To prevent session fixation attacks, regenerate the session ID upon each login:

php

```php
session_regenerate_id();
```

This step makes it harder for attackers to hijack an active session.

Logging Out

To log users out and destroy their session, use session_destroy and unset session variables:

php

```php
<?php

session_start();

session_unset();

session_destroy();

echo "You have been logged out.";

?>
```

This script clears session data and ends the user's session, logging them out of the application.

Understanding Cookies

Cookies are small pieces of data stored on the user's device, often used to remember user preferences or keep users logged in across sessions. You can set a cookie with PHP's setcookie function:

php

```php
<?php

setcookie("user_preference", "dark_mode", time() + (86400 * 30)); // 30 days

?>
```

In this example:

- user_preference is set to dark_mode.

- The cookie expires in 30 days, making it ideal for long-term storage.

To retrieve the cookie value:

php

```
echo $_COOKIE["user_preference"];
```

Cookies should only store non-sensitive data, as they're accessible to the client.

Access Control

Access control restricts certain areas of your site based on user roles and permissions. Common roles include **admin**, **editor**, and **user**, each with different levels of access.

Defining User Roles

User roles can be stored in the database as part of the user record. For example, the users table might include a role column with values like admin or user.

Example Database Schema

sql

```
CREATE TABLE users (
    id INT AUTO_INCREMENT PRIMARY KEY,
    username VARCHAR(50),
    email VARCHAR(100),
    password VARCHAR(255),
    role VARCHAR(20) DEFAULT 'user'
);
```

With this schema, you can assign a role to each user.

Implementing Access Control in PHP

To restrict access based on role, check the user's role before displaying content. Here's an example where only administrators can access a specific page:

php

```php
<?php
session_start();

if ($_SESSION['role'] !== 'admin') {
    die("Access denied.");
}
```

```php
// Admin-only content goes here

echo "Welcome, Admin!";

?>
```

This script checks if the user's role is admin. If not, access is denied, ensuring only authorized users can view the page.

Access Control Middleware

For larger applications, it's efficient to create middleware functions to handle access control across multiple pages. Here's a function that checks if a user is logged in and redirects them if they're not:

php

```php
<?php
function checkLoggedIn() {
    if (!isset($_SESSION['user_id'])) {
        header("Location: login.php");
        exit();
    }
}
?>
```

Include checkLoggedIn() at the top of any page requiring authentication, and it will redirect unauthenticated users to the login page.

Role-Based Access Control (RBAC)

RBAC is a method of restricting access based on user roles and permissions. You can implement a simple RBAC system by defining role permissions in an array or database.

php

```php
<?php
$permissions = [
    'admin' => ['view_users', 'edit_users', 'delete_users'],
    'editor' => ['view_users', 'edit_users'],
    'user' => ['view_users']
];


function hasPermission($role, $permission) {
    global $permissions;
    return in_array($permission, $permissions[$role]);
}
```

```php
// Check if the current user has permission
if (hasPermission($_SESSION['role'], 'delete_users')) {
    echo "You have permission to delete users.";
} else {
    echo "Access denied.";
}
?>
```

In this example:

- $permissions defines each role's permissions.
- hasPermission checks if a role has a specific permission, allowing fine-grained access control.

Conclusion

In this chapter, we covered essential aspects of user authentication and session management in PHP. You learned how to build a user registration and login system, secure user passwords, and manage sessions effectively. Additionally, we implemented access control mechanisms, allowing you to define roles and permissions for different areas of your application.

These techniques provide the foundation for secure, user-specific experiences and are crucial for protecting user data and restricting access. In the next chapter, we'll delve into security best practices to further safeguard your PHP applications from common vulnerabilities.

Chapter 9: Working with APIs in PHP

APIs (Application Programming Interfaces) allow applications to communicate and exchange data. In PHP, you can build your own APIs or interact with third-party APIs to integrate external data into your application. This chapter covers the basics of creating a RESTful API, consuming APIs, and working with real-world examples, such as weather and social media APIs.

RESTful API Basics

A RESTful API is an architectural style for designing networked applications. REST (Representational State Transfer) allows clients to access resources through stateless requests, typically using HTTP methods such as GET, POST, PUT, and DELETE.

Setting Up a Simple REST API in PHP

Let's create a simple REST API in PHP to manage a list of products. The API will support the following endpoints:

- GET /products: Retrieve all products

- GET /products/{id}: Retrieve a single product by ID

- POST /products: Add a new product
- PUT /products/{id}: Update a product
- DELETE /products/{id}: Delete a product

Step 1: Create the Database Table

First, create a products table in your database:

sql

```sql
CREATE TABLE products (
    id INT AUTO_INCREMENT PRIMARY KEY,
    name VARCHAR(100),
    description TEXT,
    price DECIMAL(10, 2)
);
```

Step 2: Set Up the API Endpoints

Create an api.php file to handle incoming API requests. To determine which HTTP method is being used, use $_SERVER['REQUEST_METHOD']. Based on the method, execute the corresponding functionality.

php

```php
<?php
```

```php
require 'db.php';

header("Content-Type: application/json");

$requestMethod =
$_SERVER['REQUEST_METHOD'];
switch ($requestMethod) {
    case 'GET':
        if (isset($_GET['id'])) {
            getProduct($_GET['id']);
        } else {
            getProducts();
        }
        break;
    case 'POST':
        addProduct();
        break;
    case 'PUT':
        parse_str(file_get_contents("php://input"),
$_PUT);
        updateProduct($_PUT['id']);
```

```php
        break;
    case 'DELETE':
        parse_str(file_get_contents("php://input"),
$_DELETE);
        deleteProduct($_DELETE['id']);
        break;
    default:
        echo json_encode(["message" => "Unsupported
request method"]);
}
?>
```

Here's how each function works:

- $_SERVER['REQUEST_METHOD'] checks the HTTP method.

- file_get_contents("php://input") retrieves data for PUT and DELETE requests.

Step 3: Implement the CRUD Functions

Define the functions for each operation.

Retrieve All Products (GET)

```php
php

function getProducts() {
    global $pdo;
    $stmt = $pdo->query("SELECT * FROM products");
    $products = $stmt->fetchAll(PDO::FETCH_ASSOC);
    echo json_encode($products);
}
```

Retrieve a Single Product by ID (GET)

```php
php

function getProduct($id) {
    global $pdo;
    $stmt = $pdo->prepare("SELECT * FROM products WHERE id = :id");
    $stmt->execute(['id' => $id]);
    $product = $stmt->fetch(PDO::FETCH_ASSOC);
    echo json_encode($product ? $product : ["message" => "Product not found"]);
}
```

Add a New Product (POST)

php

```php
function addProduct() {
    global $pdo;
    $data = json_decode(file_get_contents("php://input"), true);
    $stmt = $pdo->prepare("INSERT INTO products (name, description, price) VALUES (:name, :description, :price)");
    $stmt->execute([
        'name' => $data['name'],
        'description' => $data['description'],
        'price' => $data['price']
    ]);
    echo json_encode(["message" => "Product added successfully"]);
}
```

Update a Product (PUT)

php

```php
function updateProduct($id) {
```

```php
global $pdo;

$data =
json_decode(file_get_contents("php://input"), true);

$stmt = $pdo->prepare("UPDATE products SET
name = :name, description = :description, price =
:price WHERE id = :id");

$stmt->execute([

    'name' => $data['name'],

    'description' => $data['description'],

    'price' => $data['price'],

    'id' => $id

]);

echo json_encode(["message" => "Product updated
successfully"]);

}
```

Delete a Product (DELETE)

php

```php
function deleteProduct($id) {

    global $pdo;
```

```php
$stmt = $pdo->prepare("DELETE FROM products
WHERE id = :id");

$stmt->execute(['id' => $id]);

echo json_encode(["message" => "Product deleted
successfully"]);
}
```

These functions handle CRUD operations for the products table and return JSON responses. You can now test your API with tools like Postman to send requests and view responses.

Consuming APIs

PHP can also act as a client to consume external APIs. This is commonly done using the file_get_contents function or the cURL library.

Example: Fetching JSON Data with file_get_contents

Let's use file_get_contents to fetch data from an API. Here's how to retrieve data from a public API, such as the JSONPlaceholder API:

php

```php
<?php
$url = "https://jsonplaceholder.typicode.com/posts";

$response = file_get_contents($url);

$posts = json_decode($response, true);


foreach ($posts as $post) {

    echo "<h2>" . htmlspecialchars($post['title']) . "</h2>";

    echo "<p>" . htmlspecialchars($post['body']) . "</p>";

}
?>
```

In this example:

- file_get_contents retrieves data from the API.
- json_decode converts the JSON response into an associative array.

Example: Using cURL to Fetch Data

cURL offers more options for handling API requests, such as setting headers or handling different request types.

php

```php
<?php
$url = "https://jsonplaceholder.typicode.com/posts";
$ch = curl_init();

curl_setopt($ch, CURLOPT_URL, $url);
curl_setopt($ch, CURLOPT_RETURNTRANSFER,
true);

$response = curl_exec($ch);
curl_close($ch);

$posts = json_decode($response, true);

foreach ($posts as $post) {
    echo "<h2>" . htmlspecialchars($post['title']) .
"</h2>";
    echo "<p>" . htmlspecialchars($post['body']) .
"</p>";
}
?>
```

With cURL, you can also perform POST, PUT, and
DELETE requests by setting CURLOPT_POST,

CURLOPT_CUSTOMREQUEST, and
CURLOPT_POSTFIELDS.

Real-World API Examples

Let's explore some practical examples of integrating real-world APIs into a PHP application. We'll look at two popular APIs: a weather API and a social media API.

Example 1: Fetching Weather Data

To display real-time weather data, you can use the OpenWeatherMap API, which provides current weather conditions based on location.

1. **Register for an API Key**: Sign up at OpenWeatherMap to get an API key.

2. **Set Up the API Request**:

php

```php
<?php
$apiKey = "YOUR_API_KEY";
$city = "New York";
$url = "http://api.openweathermap.org/data/2.5/weather?q=$city&appid=$apiKey&units=metric";

$response = file_get_contents($url);
```

```php
$weatherData = json_decode($response, true);

if ($weatherData && $weatherData['cod'] === 200) {
    echo "<h2>Weather in " . htmlspecialchars($city) . "</h2>";

    echo "<p>Temperature: " . htmlspecialchars($weatherData['main']['temp']) . "°C</p>";

    echo "<p>Condition: " . htmlspecialchars($weatherData['weather'][0]['description']) . "</p>";
} else {
    echo "Weather data not available.";
}
?>
```

In this example:

- The API URL includes parameters for the city, API key, and units (metric).
- The temperature and weather condition are extracted from the JSON response and displayed.

Example 2: Posting to Social Media

For social media integration, many platforms, like Twitter, provide APIs for posting updates. Using

Twitter's API as an example, you can post a status update from your PHP application.

1. **Create a Twitter Developer Account**: Register and create a Twitter app at Twitter Developer to get API keys.

2. **Install the TwitterOAuth Library**: This library simplifies working with Twitter's API. You can install it with Composer:

bash

```bash
composer require abraham/twitteroauth
```

3. **Set Up the Twitter API Request**:

php

```php
<?php
require "vendor/autoload.php";
use Abraham\TwitterOAuth\TwitterOAuth;

$consumerKey = "YOUR_CONSUMER_KEY";
$consumerSecret = "YOUR_CONSUMER_SECRET";
$accessToken = "YOUR_ACCESS_TOKEN";
```

```php
$accessTokenSecret =
"YOUR_ACCESS_TOKEN_SECRET";


$twitter = new TwitterOAuth($consumerKey,
$consumerSecret, $accessToken,
$accessTokenSecret);

$status = "Hello, Twitter! #APIintegration";

$response = $twitter->post("statuses/update", ["status"
=> $status]);


if ($twitter->getLastHttpCode() == 200) {

    echo "Tweet posted successfully!";

} else {

    echo "Error posting tweet.";

}
?>
```

In this example:

- TwitterOAuth establishes an authenticated connection.

- The statuses/update endpoint posts a new status update, displaying a success message if the request succeeds.

Conclusion

In this chapter, you've learned the basics of working with APIs in PHP. You started by building a RESTful API, then explored techniques for consuming external APIs, such as using file_get_contents and cURL. Finally, we applied this knowledge with real-world examples by integrating weather data and posting to social media.

These skills allow you to connect your PHP applications with external services and bring in real-time, dynamic content, enhancing user experience and functionality. In the next chapter, we'll focus on security best practices to further protect your applications as they interact with external data and services.

Chapter 10: Advanced Database Techniques

As applications grow in complexity, so do their database requirements. Beyond basic CRUD operations, advanced techniques can improve database security, performance, and efficiency. In this chapter, we'll explore using prepared statements to prevent SQL injection, advanced SQL concepts like joins and subqueries, and optimization techniques like indexing and caching to boost database performance.

Using Prepared Statements

Prepared statements are a powerful way to enhance both the security and efficiency of database queries. A prepared statement is a query that the database compiles once, and you can execute it multiple times with different parameters, avoiding the need to parse the query each time.

Why Use Prepared Statements?

Prepared statements offer two primary benefits:

1. **Prevention of SQL Injection**: By separating SQL commands from data, prepared statements prevent attackers from injecting malicious SQL code.

2. **Optimization**: The database compiles the query once, allowing repeated execution with different values, which improves performance for repeated queries.

Implementing Prepared Statements in PHP

In PHP, prepared statements can be created using the PDO extension. Here's an example of a simple prepared statement to fetch user information securely:

php

```php
<?php
require 'db.php';

$username = $_POST['username'];
$password = $_POST['password'];


// Using a prepared statement
$sql = "SELECT * FROM users WHERE username = :username AND password = :password";

$stmt = $pdo->prepare($sql);

$stmt->execute(['username' => $username, 'password' => $password]);

$user = $stmt->fetch();
```

```php
if ($user) {

    echo "Welcome, " .
htmlspecialchars($user['username']);

} else {

    echo "Invalid credentials.";

}

?>
```

In this example:

- The placeholders :username and :password are used in the query.

- execute binds the actual values securely to these placeholders, preventing any chance of SQL injection.

- The values are safely encoded using htmlspecialchars when displayed to prevent cross-site scripting (XSS).

Best Practices for Prepared Statements

1. **Always Use Prepared Statements for User Input**: Any data that comes from users should go through a prepared statement.

2. **Use bindParam for More Control**: For more complex queries, you can use bindParam to

specify data types, which enhances security and prevents incorrect data insertion.

Advanced SQL Queries

Advanced SQL queries allow you to retrieve and manipulate data more efficiently. Let's look at a few powerful SQL techniques: joins, subqueries, and indexing.

Joins

A join combines data from two or more tables based on a related column. Joins are critical for managing complex relationships in relational databases.

Types of Joins

1. **INNER JOIN**: Returns records with matching values in both tables.

2. **LEFT JOIN**: Returns all records from the left table, with matching records from the right table, or NULL if no match exists.

3. **RIGHT JOIN**: Similar to LEFT JOIN but includes all records from the right table.

4. **FULL JOIN**: Returns records where there is a match in either table (not supported in MySQL).

Example: INNER JOIN

Suppose you have two tables, orders and customers, and you want to retrieve the order information along with customer details:

sql

```sql
SELECT orders.id, orders.order_date,
customers.name, customers.email
FROM orders
INNER JOIN customers ON orders.customer_id =
customers.id;
```

This query fetches all orders with corresponding customer names and emails, making it easy to see who placed each order.

Example: LEFT JOIN

A LEFT JOIN retrieves all orders, including those without a matching customer, which is useful for identifying records with missing information.

sql

```sql
SELECT orders.id, orders.order_date,
customers.name, customers.email
FROM orders
```

LEFT JOIN customers ON orders.customer_id = customers.id;

Subqueries

A subquery (or inner query) is a query nested within another SQL query. Subqueries are useful when you need results from multiple queries or when the data you need depends on a condition from another query.

Example: Subquery for Filtering Results

Suppose you want to find customers who have placed orders totaling more than $500:

sql

```
SELECT name FROM customers
WHERE id IN (
    SELECT customer_id FROM orders
    GROUP BY customer_id
    HAVING SUM(order_total) > 500
);
```

Here:

- The subquery groups orders by customer_id and sums the order_total for each.
- The outer query uses this list of customer_ids to filter customers who meet the condition.

Indexing

Indexes are special data structures that improve the speed of data retrieval operations on a database table at the cost of additional storage space. By indexing columns frequently used in search conditions or joins, you can significantly speed up queries.

Creating an Index

To create an index on a column, use the following SQL command:

sql

```
CREATE INDEX idx_customer_name ON customers(name);
```

In this example, an index is created on the name column in the customers table, which speeds up searches involving the customer's name.

Types of Indexes

1. **Primary Index**: Automatically created for the primary key of a table, ensuring each value is unique.

2. **Unique Index**: Ensures all values in the column are unique, often used for columns like email addresses.

3. **Composite Index**: Combines multiple columns, useful for queries that filter by multiple columns.

Best Practices for Indexing

- **Index Frequently Queried Columns**: Especially those used in WHERE, JOIN, and ORDER BY clauses.

- **Avoid Excessive Indexing**: Each index consumes storage and slows down INSERT and UPDATE operations.

- **Use Composite Indexes Judiciously**: Composite indexes can optimize specific query patterns but should only be used when queries consistently involve those columns.

Database Optimization

Optimizing your database helps improve performance, reduce load times, and ensure the scalability of your application. Let's explore some common database optimization techniques: indexing, query caching, and normalization.

Indexing for Performance

Indexes are one of the most effective ways to improve query performance, especially for large tables. When used appropriately, indexes make lookups, joins, and sort operations much faster.

Example: Optimizing a Search Query with Indexes

Imagine a table with millions of rows in an e-commerce application. Without an index, a query like the following could take a long time:

sql

SELECT * FROM products WHERE product_name = 'Laptop';

Adding an index on the product_name column speeds up this search significantly:

sql

CREATE INDEX idx_product_name ON products(product_name);

After indexing, the database uses the index to locate relevant rows quickly, making the search more efficient.

Query Caching

Query caching stores the results of frequent queries, reducing the time required to process repeat queries. While some databases have built-in caching, you can also implement caching in PHP.

Example: Simple Query Caching in PHP

Here's a PHP example that uses file-based caching for a frequently run query:

php

```php
<?php
$cacheFile = 'cache/products.json';
$cacheTime = 60 * 5; // 5 minutes

if (file_exists($cacheFile) && (time() -
filemtime($cacheFile) < $cacheTime)) {
    $products =
json_decode(file_get_contents($cacheFile), true);
} else {
    $stmt = $pdo->query("SELECT * FROM
products");
    $products = $stmt-
>fetchAll(PDO::FETCH_ASSOC);
    file_put_contents($cacheFile,
json_encode($products));
}

foreach ($products as $product) {
    echo "<h2>" . htmlspecialchars($product['name']) .
"</h2>";
```

```php
    echo "<p>Price: $" .
htmlspecialchars($product['price']) . "</p>";

}

?>
```

In this example:

- The cache file is checked for freshness.

- If it's still valid, data is loaded from the cache; otherwise, a fresh query is run and results are saved in the cache.

Database Normalization

Normalization is the process of organizing data to reduce redundancy and improve integrity. Following normalization principles, you divide data into tables and link them through relationships. The three normal forms (1NF, 2NF, and 3NF) are the most commonly used:

1. **First Normal Form (1NF)**: Ensure that each column contains atomic (indivisible) values.

2. **Second Normal Form (2NF)**: Each column depends on the primary key.

3. **Third Normal Form (3NF)**: Remove columns that depend on non-primary key attributes.

Example: Normalization in Practice

Suppose you have an unnormalized orders table where each row contains customer details. To normalize:

1. Create a separate customers table for customer information.
2. Store only a reference to the customer_id in the orders table.

sql

```sql
CREATE TABLE customers (
    id INT AUTO_INCREMENT PRIMARY KEY,
    name VARCHAR(50),
    email VARCHAR(100)
);


CREATE TABLE orders (
    id INT AUTO_INCREMENT PRIMARY KEY,
    customer_id INT,
    order_total DECIMAL(10, 2),
    FOREIGN KEY (customer_id) REFERENCES customers(id)
);
```

By splitting data into multiple tables, normalization reduces redundancy, which improves data consistency and minimizes storage requirements.

Conclusion

In this chapter, we explored advanced database techniques essential for building efficient, scalable applications. Prepared statements improve both security and performance by preventing SQL injection. Advanced SQL queries, including joins, subqueries, and indexing, enable efficient data retrieval and manipulation. Finally, database optimization techniques, such as indexing, caching, and normalization, ensure your application can handle large datasets and complex queries with ease.

With these techniques, you're now equipped to build robust, secure, and high-performance database-driven applications. The next chapter will focus on testing and debugging PHP applications, helping you ensure reliability as you scale your projects

Chapter 11: PHP and JavaScript for Dynamic Websites

Combining PHP and JavaScript allows you to build highly interactive, responsive web applications. While PHP runs on the server, JavaScript operates on the client side, creating a seamless experience for users. In this chapter, we'll explore how to integrate PHP with JavaScript, use AJAX for asynchronous interactions, and leverage Websockets to enable real-time communication. By the end, you'll be able to create websites that dynamically respond to user actions without constant page reloads.

Integrating PHP with JavaScript

PHP and JavaScript operate on different layers of the web stack: PHP processes requests on the server, while JavaScript handles interactions in the browser. Integrating the two enables data exchange between the client and server, making pages more interactive.

Example 1: Passing Data from PHP to JavaScript

One common scenario is passing PHP data to JavaScript, such as user information or site settings that need to be available on the client side.

Embedding PHP Data in JavaScript

Here's an example where a PHP script passes user data to JavaScript:

php

```php
<?php
// Sample PHP data
$user = [
    'id' => 123,
    'name' => 'Alice',
    'email' => 'alice@example.com'
];
?>
```

```html
<!DOCTYPE html>
<html lang="en">
<head>
    <meta charset="UTF-8">
    <title>PHP and JavaScript Integration</title>
```

```html
</head>
<body>

<script>
    // Pass PHP data to JavaScript by encoding it as JSON
    const user = <?php echo json_encode($user); ?>;
    console.log("User ID:", user.id); // Outputs: User ID: 123
</script>

</body>
</html>
```

In this example:

- json_encode($user) converts the PHP array into a JSON object.

- JavaScript can access the user object and log its properties.

Example 2: Sending Data from JavaScript to PHP

You may also need to send data from JavaScript to PHP, often done via AJAX requests. Here's how to use JavaScript's fetch API to send data to a PHP script:

html

```html
<!DOCTYPE html>
<html lang="en">
<head>
  <meta charset="UTF-8">
  <title>JavaScript to PHP</title>
</head>
<body>

<button id="saveButton">Save Data</button>

<script>

document.getElementById('saveButton').addEventListener('click', () => {
    const data = { userId: 123, action: 'save' };

    fetch('process_data.php', {
      method: 'POST',
      headers: {
```

```
          'Content-Type': 'application/json'
        },
      body: JSON.stringify(data)
    })
    .then(response => response.json())
    .then(data => console.log('Response:', data))
    .catch(error => console.error('Error:', error));
  });
</script>

</body>
</html>
```

In process_data.php:

php

```php
<?php
// Retrieve JSON data from the request
$data = json_decode(file_get_contents("php://input"),
true);


// Process the data and send a response
```

```php
$response = [

    'status' => 'success',

    'message' => 'Data received and processed',

    'userId' => $data['userId']

];


echo json_encode($response);

?>
```

In this example:

- JavaScript sends data using fetch with the POST method.

- process_data.php receives and decodes the JSON data, processes it, and sends a JSON response back to JavaScript.

AJAX for Asynchronous Interactions

AJAX (Asynchronous JavaScript and XML) allows you to send and receive data from the server without reloading the page. This technique is essential for creating dynamic, interactive websites where data updates instantly in response to user actions.

How AJAX Works

AJAX uses JavaScript's XMLHttpRequest or fetch API to send asynchronous requests to the server. The server processes the request and sends a response, which JavaScript then processes to update the page.

Example: Loading Data with AJAX

Suppose you're building a blog page where comments load dynamically without reloading the page.

1. **JavaScript AJAX Request**:

html

```
<!DOCTYPE html>
<html lang="en">
<head>
    <meta charset="UTF-8">
    <title>AJAX Example</title>
</head>
<body>


<h2>Blog Post</h2>
<p>This is a blog post with comments loaded asynchronously.</p>
```

```html
<button id="loadComments">Load Comments</button>

<div id="comments"></div>


<script>

document.getElementById('loadComments').addEventListener('click', () => {
    fetch('fetch_comments.php')
        .then(response => response.json())
        .then(comments => {
            const commentsDiv = document.getElementById('comments');
            commentsDiv.innerHTML = ''; // Clear previous comments
            comments.forEach(comment => {
                const commentElement = document.createElement('p');
                commentElement.textContent = comment.text;

                commentsDiv.appendChild(commentElement);
```

```
            });
        })
        .catch(error => console.error('Error:', error));
    });
</script>


</body>
</html>
```

2. **PHP Script (fetch_comments.php)**:

php

```php
<?php
// Simulate fetching comments from a database
$comments = [
    ['text' => 'Great post!'],
    ['text' => 'Very informative. Thanks!'],
    ['text' => 'Looking forward to more posts.']
];

// Return comments as JSON
echo json_encode($comments);
```

?>

In this example:

- The fetch_comments.php script returns comments in JSON format.
- JavaScript's fetch function retrieves the comments and updates the comments section dynamically.

Submitting Forms with AJAX

AJAX can also handle form submissions without reloading the page. Here's how to use AJAX for a simple contact form:

1. **Contact Form**:

html

```html
<form id="contactForm">
    <input type="text" name="name" placeholder="Your Name" required>
    <input type="email" name="email" placeholder="Your Email" required>
    <textarea name="message" placeholder="Your Message" required></textarea>
    <button type="submit">Send Message</button>
</form>
```

```html
<div id="response"></div>

<script>

document.getElementById('contactForm').addEventLis
tener('submit', event => {
    event.preventDefault();

    const formData = new FormData(event.target);

    fetch('process_contact.php', {
      method: 'POST',
      body: formData
    })
    .then(response => response.text())
    .then(data => {

document.getElementById('response').textContent =
data;
    })
    .catch(error => console.error('Error:', error));
  });
```

</script>

2. **PHP Script (process_contact.php)**:

php

```php
<?php
$name = $_POST['name'];
$email = $_POST['email'];
$message = $_POST['message'];

echo "Thank you, $name! Your message has been received.";
?>
```

In this example:

- The form data is sent to process_contact.php via AJAX.

- The PHP script processes the data and returns a response, which JavaScript displays without a page reload.

Websockets and Real-Time Data

Websockets enable real-time communication between the client and server, making it possible to build applications like chat rooms, live notifications, and collaborative tools. Unlike AJAX, which requires repeated requests, Websockets maintain a persistent connection, allowing instant data exchange.

Setting Up a Simple WebSocket Server in PHP

To use Websockets with PHP, you'll need a WebSocket server. Let's use Ratchet, a popular WebSocket library for PHP.

1. **Install Ratchet**: Install Ratchet using Composer:

bash

```
composer require cboden/ratchet
```

2. **Create a WebSocket Server (server.php)**:

php

```php
<?php
use Ratchet\MessageComponentInterface;
use Ratchet\ConnectionInterface;

require 'vendor/autoload.php';

class ChatServer implements MessageComponentInterface {
```

```php
    protected $clients;

    public function __construct() {
        $this->clients = new \SplObjectStorage;
    }

    public function onOpen(ConnectionInterface $conn) {
        $this->clients->attach($conn);
        echo "New connection! ({$conn->resourceId})\n";
    }

    public function onMessage(ConnectionInterface $from, $msg) {
        foreach ($this->clients as $client) {
            if ($from !== $client) {
                $client->send($msg);
            }
        }
    }
```

```php
    public function onClose(ConnectionInterface $conn)
    {
        $this->clients->detach($conn);

        echo "Connection {$conn->resourceId} has disconnected\n";

    }


    public function onError(ConnectionInterface $conn, \Exception $e) {

        echo "An error has occurred: {$e->getMessage()}\n";

        $conn->close();

    }

}


$server = Ratchet\App('localhost', 8080);

$server->route('/chat', new ChatServer, ['*']);

$server->run();

?>
```

This WebSocket server allows multiple clients to connect and exchange messages in real time. When one client sends a message, it's broadcast to all other connected clients.

Building a Simple Chat Client with JavaScript

To connect to this WebSocket server, create an HTML page with JavaScript to send and receive messages.

html

```html
<!DOCTYPE html>
<html lang="en">
<head>
    <meta charset="UTF-8">
    <title>WebSocket Chat</title>
</head>
<body>

    <h2>WebSocket Chat</h2>
    <div id="messages"></div>
    <input type="text" id="messageInput" placeholder="Type a message">
    <button id="sendMessage">Send</button>

    <script>
        const ws = new WebSocket('ws://localhost:8080/chat');
```

```
ws.onopen = () => {

    console.log("Connected to WebSocket server");

};


ws.onmessage = event => {

    const messagesDiv =
document.getElementById('messages');

    const messageElement =
document.createElement('p');

        messageElement.textContent = event.data;

        messagesDiv.appendChild(messageElement);

};


document.getElementById('sendMessage').addEventLi
stener('click', () => {

    const messageInput =
document.getElementById('messageInput');

        ws.send(messageInput.value);

        messageInput.value = '';

});
```

```
</script>
```

```
</body>
```

```
</html>
```

In this example:

- JavaScript connects to the WebSocket server on ws://localhost:8080/chat.

- Messages sent by one client are broadcast to all connected clients, creating a basic chat room.

Conclusion

In this chapter, we covered the powerful combination of PHP and JavaScript to create dynamic web applications. You learned how to integrate PHP with JavaScript, use AJAX for asynchronous data loading, and set up Websockets for real-time communication. These techniques allow you to build highly interactive, responsive websites that provide an excellent user experience.

With these tools, you're now equipped to create real-time, data-driven applications that go beyond simple page refreshes. In the next chapter, we'll dive into testing and debugging, essential skills for ensuring your applications function reliably and efficiently.

Chapter 12: Building a Simple CMS (Content Management System)

A Content Management System (CMS) allows users to manage website content without needing to modify code directly. Many popular platforms, like WordPress, are CMS-based, enabling non-technical users to create, edit, and organize content. In this chapter, we'll build a basic CMS using PHP, focusing on backend development for content and user management, then integrating it with a frontend layout to display dynamic, database-driven content.

Project Overview

CMS Features

Our CMS will have three core features:

1. **User Management**: Users can register, log in, and manage their accounts. An admin user can add, edit, and delete users.

2. **Content Management**: Users can create, edit, and delete articles, which include a title, body, and author.

3. **Frontend Display**: Articles will be displayed on the website, with templates for a consistent layout.

Database Structure

The CMS will use two main tables in the database:

1. **Users**: Stores information about each user, including login credentials and role (e.g., admin or editor).

2. **Articles**: Stores article content, including the title, body, and a reference to the author.

Example Database Schema

sql

```sql
CREATE TABLE users (
    id INT AUTO_INCREMENT PRIMARY KEY,
    username VARCHAR(50) UNIQUE NOT NULL,
    password VARCHAR(255) NOT NULL,
    role ENUM('admin', 'editor') DEFAULT 'editor'
);

CREATE TABLE articles (
    id INT AUTO_INCREMENT PRIMARY KEY,
```

```
    title VARCHAR(255) NOT NULL,

    body TEXT NOT NULL,

    author_id INT,

    created_at TIMESTAMP DEFAULT
CURRENT_TIMESTAMP,

    FOREIGN KEY (author_id) REFERENCES
users(id)

);
```

- **Users Table**: Holds user credentials and role.
- **Articles Table**: Stores each article's title, content, author, and timestamp.

Backend Development

User Management

User management includes registration, login, and assigning user roles. Let's start by creating a registration form, handling user login, and setting up role-based access control.

User Registration

Create a registration form in register.php and a processing script to handle form submissions securely.

Registration Form (register.php):

html

```html
<form action="process_register.php" method="post">
    <label for="username">Username:</label>
    <input type="text" name="username" id="username" required>

    <label for="password">Password:</label>
    <input type="password" name="password" id="password" required>

    <button type="submit">Register</button>
</form>
```

Processing Script (process_register.php):

php

```php
<?php
require 'db.php';

$username = $_POST['username'];
$password = password_hash($_POST['password'], PASSWORD_DEFAULT);
```

```php
$role = 'editor'; // Default role


$sql = "INSERT INTO users (username, password, role) VALUES (:username, :password, :role)";

$stmt = $pdo->prepare($sql);

$stmt->execute(['username' => $username, 'password' => $password, 'role' => $role]);


echo "Registration successful!";
?>
```

In this script:

- The password is hashed for security.
- The user is given a default editor role, which limits access compared to an admin.
-

User Login and Role-Based Access

Create a login form (login.php) and a processing script to authenticate users.

Login Form (login.php):

html


```html
<form action="process_login.php" method="post">
```

```html
<label for="username">Username:</label>
<input type="text" name="username" id="username" required>

<label for="password">Password:</label>
<input type="password" name="password" id="password" required>

<button type="submit">Login</button>
</form>
```

Processing Script (process_login.php):

php

```php
<?php
session_start();
require 'db.php';

$username = $_POST['username'];
$password = $_POST['password'];

$sql = "SELECT * FROM users WHERE username = :username";
```

```php
$stmt = $pdo->prepare($sql);

$stmt->execute(['username' => $username]);

$user = $stmt->fetch();


if ($user && password_verify($password,
$user['password'])) {

    $_SESSION['user_id'] = $user['id'];

    $_SESSION['username'] = $user['username'];

    $_SESSION['role'] = $user['role'];

    echo "Login successful!";
} else {

    echo "Invalid username or password.";

}
?>
```

In this example:

- User credentials are validated, and if successful, the session is started.

- Role-based access can be enforced later by checking $_SESSION['role'].

Content Management (CRUD for Articles)

Articles represent the main content in this CMS. Users with the appropriate permissions can create, edit, and delete articles.

Creating an Article

Create a form to add a new article, then process the submission to store it in the database.

Article Form (add_article.php):

html

```
<form action="process_add_article.php" method="post">

    <label for="title">Title:</label>

    <input type="text" name="title" id="title" required>


    <label for="body">Content:</label>

    <textarea name="body" id="body" required></textarea>


    <button type="submit">Add Article</button>
</form>
```

Processing Script (process_add_article.php):

php

```php
<?php
session_start();
require 'db.php';

$title = $_POST['title'];
$body = $_POST['body'];
$author_id = $_SESSION['user_id'];

$sql = "INSERT INTO articles (title, body, author_id) VALUES (:title, :body, :author_id)";
$stmt = $pdo->prepare($sql);
$stmt->execute(['title' => $title, 'body' => $body, 'author_id' => $author_id]);

echo "Article added successfully!";
?>
```

This script:

- Inserts a new article into the articles table with a reference to the author's user_id.

- Ensures only logged-in users can add articles.

Editing and Deleting Articles

For editing articles, create a form populated with existing article data and update the article in the database.

Editing an Article (edit_article.php):

php

```php
<?php
require 'db.php';
$article_id = $_GET['id'];
$stmt = $pdo->prepare("SELECT * FROM articles WHERE id = :id");
$stmt->execute(['id' => $article_id]);
$article = $stmt->fetch();
?>
```

```html
<form action="process_edit_article.php" method="post">
    <input type="hidden" name="id" value="<?php echo htmlspecialchars($article['id']); ?>">
    <label for="title">Title:</label>
```

```html
<input type="text" name="title" value="<?php echo
htmlspecialchars($article['title']); ?>" required>

<label for="body">Content:</label>

<textarea name="body" required><?php echo
htmlspecialchars($article['body']); ?></textarea>

<button type="submit">Update Article</button>
</form>
```

Processing Script (process_edit_article.php):

php

```php
<?php
require 'db.php';

$id = $_POST['id'];
$title = $_POST['title'];
$body = $_POST['body'];

$sql = "UPDATE articles SET title = :title, body =
:body WHERE id = :id";
$stmt = $pdo->prepare($sql);
```

```php
$stmt->execute(['title' => $title, 'body' => $body, 'id' => $id]);

echo "Article updated successfully!";
?>
```

For deleting articles, confirm the deletion request and delete the record from the database:

php

```php
<?php
require 'db.php';
$article_id = $_POST['id'];

$sql = "DELETE FROM articles WHERE id = :id";
$stmt = $pdo->prepare($sql);
$stmt->execute(['id' => $article_id]);

echo "Article deleted successfully.";
?>
```

Frontend Integration

The frontend of the CMS displays articles, with templates for consistent styling across pages. Templates enable separation of content from layout, simplifying maintenance and improving readability.

Displaying Articles on the Homepage

Create a home.php file that retrieves articles from the database and displays them with a simple layout.

Homepage Template (home.php):

php

```php
<!DOCTYPE html>
<html lang="en">
<head>
    <meta charset="UTF-8">
    <title>Simple CMS</title>
</head>
<body>
    <h1>Welcome to the CMS</h1>
    <h2>Articles</h2>

    <?php
```

```php
require 'db.php';

$stmt = $pdo->query("SELECT articles.*,
users.username FROM articles JOIN users ON
articles.author_id = users.id ORDER BY created_at
DESC");

while ($article = $stmt->fetch()) {

    echo "<h3>" . htmlspecialchars($article['title']) .
"</h3>";

    echo "<p>By " .
htmlspecialchars($article['username']) . " on " .
$article['created_at'] . "</p>";

    echo "<p>" .
nl2br(htmlspecialchars($article['body'])) . "</p>";

}

?>
</body>
</html>
```

In this example:

- The JOIN statement retrieves the article along with the author's username.

- Articles are displayed in descending order based on creation time.

Using Templates for Consistency

Create a template.php file that contains the header and footer layout. This file will be included on each page, making the CMS layout consistent.

Template File (template.php):

php

```
<!DOCTYPE html>
<html lang="en">
<head>
    <meta charset="UTF-8">
    <title>Simple CMS</title>
    <link rel="stylesheet" href="styles.css">
</head>
<body>
    <header>
        <h1>Content Management System</h1>
        <nav>
            <a href="home.php">Home</a>
            <a href="add_article.php">Add Article</a>
            <a href="logout.php">Logout</a>
        </nav>
```

```html
  </header>

  <main>
    <?php include($content); ?>
  </main>

  <footer>
    <p>&copy; 2023 Simple CMS</p>
  </footer>
</body>
</html>
```

In each page, define $content as the page-specific content file, then include template.php:

php

```php
<?php
$content = 'home_content.php';

include 'template.php';

?>
```

Conclusion

In this chapter, you built a simple CMS that allows users to manage content and view articles dynamically on a website. Starting with the project layout, you implemented core CMS features, including user management, CRUD operations for articles, and frontend templates for a consistent layout. With these techniques, you can expand the CMS by adding features like media uploads, categories, and advanced user permissions. This CMS project provides a strong foundation for building scalable, content-driven applications in PHP.

Chapter 13: Security Best Practices

Web applications are frequently targeted by attackers looking to exploit vulnerabilities, making security a critical aspect of web development. In this chapter, we'll cover common security vulnerabilities, methods for securing input and output, and best practices for authentication and password storage. By following these security guidelines, you can protect your PHP applications and the data of your users.

Common Security Vulnerabilities

Three of the most prevalent web application vulnerabilities are Cross-Site Scripting (XSS), Cross-Site Request Forgery (CSRF), and SQL Injection. Let's explore each of these and how to defend against them.

Cross-Site Scripting (XSS)

XSS occurs when an attacker injects malicious scripts into a website that other users then view and execute in their browsers. XSS attacks can lead to data theft, session hijacking, and even control over user accounts.

Example of XSS

Consider an application where users can post comments. If input is not sanitized, an attacker could inject JavaScript into a comment field like this:

html

```
<script>alert('Hacked!');</script>
```

If displayed without encoding, this script would execute in other users' browsers.

Preventing XSS

1. **Sanitize User Input**: Use PHP's htmlspecialchars() function to encode special characters, preventing JavaScript from running in the browser.

php

```php
echo htmlspecialchars($comment, ENT_QUOTES, 'UTF-8');
```

2. **Content Security Policy (CSP)**: Configure your server to limit the types of content it loads, blocking unauthorized scripts.

php

```php
header("Content-Security-Policy: default-src 'self'");
```

By encoding user-generated content and setting a CSP header, you prevent attackers from injecting executable scripts into your application.

Cross-Site Request Forgery (CSRF)

CSRF occurs when an attacker tricks a logged-in user into performing an action they didn't intend. For example, if a user is logged into a banking application and an attacker convinces them to click on a malicious link, the user might unknowingly transfer money.

Example of CSRF

An attacker could create a hidden form that submits a money transfer request:

html

```html
<form action="https://bank.com/transfer" method="post" id="csrfForm">

    <input type="hidden" name="account" value="attackerAccount">

    <input type="hidden" name="amount" value="1000">

</form>

<script>document.getElementById('csrfForm').submit();</script>
```

If the user is logged in, the bank server might process the request as legitimate.

Preventing CSRF

1. **CSRF Tokens**: Generate a unique token for each form and verify it on submission to ensure requests are intentional.

Generating a CSRF Token:

php

```php
session_start();
if (empty($_SESSION['csrf_token'])) {
    $_SESSION['csrf_token'] = bin2hex(random_bytes(32));
}
```

Including the Token in Forms:

html

```html
<form action="transfer.php" method="post">
    <input type="hidden" name="csrf_token" value="<?php echo $_SESSION['csrf_token']; ?>">
    <!-- Other form fields -->
</form>
```

Validating the Token on Submission:

php

```php
session_start();

if ($_POST['csrf_token'] !==
$_SESSION['csrf_token']) {

    die('Invalid CSRF token');

}
```

2. **SameSite Cookies**: Use SameSite attribute on session cookies to limit them to same-origin requests, which blocks CSRF in most browsers.

php

```php
setcookie("session", $sessionId, ["samesite" =>
"Strict"]);
```

SQL Injection

SQL Injection occurs when an attacker manipulates SQL queries by injecting malicious SQL code. This vulnerability allows attackers to access, modify, or delete sensitive data.

Example of SQL Injection

Consider an application that retrieves user information based on a username:

php

$username = $_GET['username'];

$sql = "SELECT * FROM users WHERE username = '$username'";

If an attacker inputs admin' OR '1'='1, the query becomes:

sql

SELECT * FROM users WHERE username = 'admin' OR '1'='1';

This query always returns true, potentially revealing all users' data.

Preventing SQL Injection

1. **Prepared Statements**: Use prepared statements and parameterized queries, which separate SQL code from data, preventing injection.

php

```
$stmt = $pdo->prepare("SELECT * FROM users WHERE username = :username");

$stmt->execute(['username' => $username]);
```

2. **Sanitize Input**: Even when using prepared statements, always validate and sanitize input to reduce the risk of unintended behavior.

By consistently using prepared statements, you protect your application from SQL injection attacks.

Securing Input and Output

Securing input and output is critical in preventing attacks and protecting data. Best practices include validating all data, encoding output, and handling sensitive information with care.

Input Validation

Validation ensures that user input meets expected formats and constraints before it's processed.

1. **Use Built-In Filters**: PHP's filter_var function provides a range of filters for common validation tasks, such as checking for valid email addresses.

php

```php
$email = filter_var($_POST['email'], FILTER_VALIDATE_EMAIL);
```

2. **Enforce Data Types**: Define data types and patterns for expected input, such as integer-only values for age fields or specific string formats for usernames.

php

```php
$age = filter_var($_POST['age'],
FILTER_VALIDATE_INT);
```

3. **Reject Invalid Input**: If input doesn't meet validation criteria, reject it with an appropriate error message, never accepting or processing unvalidated data.

Output Encoding

Encoding prevents the display of malicious data by converting special characters into HTML entities.

1. **Use htmlspecialchars**: Always encode output when displaying user-generated content.

php

```php
echo htmlspecialchars($userInput, ENT_QUOTES,
'UTF-8');
```

2. **Use json_encode**: When sending data in JSON format, use json_encode to ensure special characters are escaped.

php

```php
echo json_encode($data);
```

By encoding output consistently, you protect your application from XSS attacks and data manipulation.

Authentication and Password Storage

Secure authentication and password storage are essential to protect user accounts. Passwords should be stored in a way that makes it difficult for attackers to retrieve them, even if they gain access to the database.

Secure Password Hashing

Storing passwords as plain text is highly insecure. Instead, use strong, one-way hashing algorithms designed for passwords.

1. **Password Hashing with password_hash**: PHP's password_hash function uses a secure algorithm (default: bcrypt) to hash passwords.

php

```php
$hashedPassword = password_hash($password, PASSWORD_DEFAULT);
```

2. **Verifying Passwords with password_verify**: Use password_verify to compare a user's input with the stored hash during login.

php

```php
if (password_verify($password, $storedHash)) {

    // Password is correct

}
```

3. **Password Rehashing**: As algorithms improve, you may need to rehash stored passwords. Use password_needs_rehash to determine if a password needs to be rehashed.

php

```php
if (password_needs_rehash($storedHash, PASSWORD_DEFAULT)) {

    $newHash = password_hash($password, PASSWORD_DEFAULT);

}
```

Account Protection and Rate Limiting

To further secure authentication, implement measures to prevent brute-force attacks and unauthorized access attempts.

1. **Rate Limiting**: Limit login attempts to prevent automated scripts from guessing passwords.

php

```
// Track failed attempts in the database and restrict
login after several failures
```

2. **Account Locking**: Temporarily lock accounts
    after multiple failed attempts to prevent
    attackers from repeatedly trying passwords.

3. **Two-Factor Authentication (2FA)**: Enhance
    security by requiring a second authentication
    factor, such as a code sent via SMS or email.

Session Security

Sessions maintain user authentication between
requests. Protect sessions with secure handling of
session cookies and proper session management.

1. **Use Secure Cookies**: Set cookies with the
    Secure and HttpOnly attributes to prevent
    access from JavaScript and enforce HTTPS-
    only transmission.

php

```php
session_set_cookie_params(['secure' => true, 'httponly' => true]);
```

2. **Regenerate Session IDs**: To prevent session
    fixation attacks, regenerate the session ID after
    logging in.

php

session_regenerate_id(true);

3. **Expire Sessions**: Implement automatic session expiration after a period of inactivity to reduce the risk of unauthorized access.

php

```
// Expire session if inactive for a specified period
if (isset($_SESSION['last_activity']) && (time() - $_SESSION['last_activity']) > 1800) {

    session_unset();

    session_destroy();

}
$_SESSION['last_activity'] = time();
```

By following these session management practices, you can protect users' session data from theft and unauthorized use.

Conclusion

In this chapter, we covered critical security best practices to safeguard PHP applications. By understanding common vulnerabilities, such as XSS, CSRF, and SQL injection, you can implement strategies to prevent them. Securing input and output with validation and encoding reduces exposure to attacks, while secure password storage and strong authentication practices protect user accounts. Finally, proper session management ensures that user sessions remain safe from interception or misuse.

Implementing these practices creates a more secure application environment, helping protect both your users and your application from common security threats. In the next chapter, we'll focus on testing and debugging, essential skills for ensuring your application's reliability as it grows in complexity.

Chapter 14: Testing and Debugging PHP Applications

Building a PHP application is only the first step; ensuring it works correctly and efficiently is essential for a successful project. This chapter covers debugging techniques, unit testing with PHPUnit, and performance optimization strategies. With these tools, you'll be able to identify and fix issues, automate testing for reliable code, and enhance your application's speed and efficiency.

Debugging Techniques

Debugging is the process of identifying and resolving issues in code. Effective debugging not only saves time but also improves code quality.

1. Using PHP's Built-In Error Reporting

PHP's error reporting features provide information about syntax errors, warnings, and notices, which help you identify problematic code.

1. **Enable Error Reporting**: Use error_reporting(E_ALL) and

ini_set('display_errors', 1) to show all errors during development.

php

```php
error_reporting(E_ALL);

ini_set('display_errors', 1);
```

2. **Log Errors to a File**: For production environments, disable error display and log errors instead to avoid revealing sensitive information to users.

php

```php
ini_set('display_errors', 0);

ini_set('log_errors', 1);

ini_set('error_log', 'path/to/error_log.txt');
```

2. Using var_dump() and print_r()

var_dump() and print_r() are simple yet effective tools to inspect variable values and data structures.

- **var_dump()**: Provides detailed information, including data type and length, which is especially useful for debugging complex data structures like arrays and objects.

php

```php
$data = ['name' => 'Alice', 'age' => 30];

var_dump($data);
```

- **print_r()**: Displays a more readable output for arrays and objects but provides less detail than var_dump().

php

```php
print_r($data);
```

Using these functions temporarily in your code helps you understand what data is being processed and detect unexpected values.

3. Using Breakpoints and Step Debugging

Breakpoints allow you to pause the execution of code and inspect its state line by line. Xdebug, a popular PHP extension, provides step debugging features that integrate with IDEs like VSCode and PHPStorm.

1. **Install Xdebug**: Install Xdebug as a PHP extension on your local server.

2. **Set Breakpoints**: In your IDE, set breakpoints at specific lines of code.

3. **Inspect Variables**: Use the IDE's debug tools to examine variables, view the call stack, and navigate through the code.

Step debugging enables you to follow the flow of execution and see precisely where issues arise.

4. Error Logging and Monitoring

Error logging enables you to track issues in production without interrupting the user experience. Use error_log() to write messages to a log file for analysis.

php

```php
if (!$result) {

    error_log("Database query failed: " . $db->error);

}
```

Many logging libraries, such as Monolog, provide more advanced features like logging levels and integration with remote logging services, giving you greater control over error tracking and monitoring.

Unit Testing with PHPUnit

Unit testing involves testing individual units of code, typically functions or methods, to ensure they work as expected. PHPUnit, a widely used PHP testing framework, automates testing, improving code reliability and making it easier to identify bugs.

Installing PHPUnit

Install PHPUnit using Composer by running the following command in your project directory:

bash

composer require --dev phpunit/phpunit

Writing Your First Unit Test

Unit tests involve setting up test cases, defining expected outcomes, and asserting that your code produces these outcomes.

Example: Testing a Calculator Class

Consider a simple Calculator class that adds two numbers:

php

```php
// Calculator.php
class Calculator {
    public function add($a, $b) {
        return $a + $b;
    }
}
```

To test this class, create a test file named CalculatorTest.php in the tests directory:

php

```php
// tests/CalculatorTest.php
use PHPUnit\Framework\TestCase;

class CalculatorTest extends TestCase {
    public function testAdd() {
        $calculator = new Calculator();
        $this->assertEquals(5, $calculator->add(2, 3));
        $this->assertEquals(0, $calculator->add(0, 0));
    }
}
```

In this example:

- **Test Case**: CalculatorTest extends TestCase, the base class for all PHPUnit test cases.

- **Assertions**: assertEquals checks if the output matches the expected value, in this case, that add(2, 3) returns 5.

Run the test with:

bash

```bash
vendor/bin/phpunit tests/CalculatorTest.php
```

If the test passes, you'll see a success message; otherwise, PHPUnit will indicate which tests failed.

Common Assertions in PHPUnit

PHPUnit offers many assertions to validate different types of data and behaviors:

- **assertTrue($condition)**: Passes if $condition is true.

- **assertFalse($condition)**: Passes if $condition is false.

- **assertNull($variable)**: Passes if $variable is null.

- **assertInstanceOf($class, $object)**: Passes if $object is an instance of $class.

Using a variety of assertions lets you test different aspects of your code thoroughly.

Test Suites and Coverage

Organize your tests into suites to group related tests together. Code coverage reports show how much of your code is tested, identifying untested areas.

- **Creating a Test Suite**: Add multiple test files in the tests directory and run them together:

bash

```
vendor/bin/phpunit --coverage-text tests
```

- **Coverage Report**: Use --coverage-text or --coverage-html to generate reports on code coverage. Ensuring a high coverage percentage helps identify parts of your codebase that may be at risk of bugs.

Unit testing with PHPUnit ensures each part of your application functions as expected and that any changes don't inadvertently break existing functionality.

Performance Optimization

Optimizing PHP applications for performance improves speed, reduces server load, and provides a smoother user experience. Let's explore key performance optimization techniques: caching, memory management, and reducing server response times.

1. Caching

Caching stores frequently accessed data temporarily, so the server doesn't need to repeatedly retrieve or process it. PHP supports several caching mechanisms.

a. Opcode Caching with Opcache

Opcache stores precompiled PHP scripts in memory, reducing the need to parse and compile scripts on every request.

1. **Enable Opcache**: Add the following settings to your php.ini file:

ini

opcache.enable=1

opcache.memory_consumption=128

opcache.max_accelerated_files=10000

2. **Check Opcache Status**: Use opcache_get_status() to monitor caching performance.

Opcache improves performance by reducing redundant compilation and processing time.

b. Data Caching with Memcached or Redis

Memcached and Redis store frequently accessed data in memory, reducing database load for repeated queries.

1. **Install Memcached or Redis**: Install Memcached or Redis on your server.

2. **Cache Database Results**: Store query results in memory and retrieve them instead of querying the database every time.

php

```
$key = "user_data_$userId";
```

```php
$data = $cache->get($key);

if (!$data) {

    $data = $db->query("SELECT * FROM users WHERE id = $userId")->fetch();

    $cache->set($key, $data, 300); // Cache for 5 minutes
}
```

By caching data that doesn't change often, you reduce database load and improve response times.

2. Optimizing Memory Usage

Memory management prevents your application from using excessive server memory, which can lead to slowdowns or even crashes.

1. **Use unset() to Free Memory**: After processing large variables, free up memory with unset().

php

```php
$data = getLargeData();

// Process data

unset($data); // Free memory
```

2. **Reduce Array and Object Size**: Avoid loading unnecessary data into memory. Retrieve only the fields you need from the database.

php

```php
// Instead of SELECT *, specify only necessary columns

$stmt = $pdo->prepare("SELECT name, email FROM users WHERE id = :id");
```

3. **Optimize Loops**: Avoid creating new variables or performing heavy operations inside loops, as this consumes more memory.

3. Minimizing Server Response Time

Server response time depends on both PHP processing time and database interaction speed. Here are techniques to reduce response time:

1. **Optimize SQL Queries**: Efficient queries speed up data retrieval. Use indexes, avoid unnecessary joins, and only request data you need.

sql

```sql
SELECT name, email FROM users WHERE id = :id;
```

2. **Use HTTP/2 or HTTP/3**: Modern HTTP protocols allow faster communication between server and client, reducing page load times.

3. **Enable GZIP Compression**: Compressing responses reduces file sizes, speeding up data transfer. Enable GZIP in your server configuration.

apache

```
# In .htaccess for Apache servers
AddOutputFilterByType DEFLATE text/html
text/plain text/xml text/css text/javascript
```

4. **Limit External Requests**: Each external request (like a third-party API call) increases response time. Minimize these calls, or cache results if data doesn't change frequently.

By implementing these optimization techniques, you can significantly improve the performance of your PHP application, leading to faster response times and better scalability.

Conclusion

In this chapter, we explored the essentials of testing and debugging PHP applications. Debugging techniques, such as error reporting, variable inspection, and step debugging, help you identify and resolve issues quickly. PHPUnit provides a framework for unit testing, enabling you to write automated tests that improve code reliability. Finally, performance optimization techniques like caching, memory management, and response time reduction enhance your application's speed and scalability.

These skills ensure that your PHP applications are robust, efficient, and maintainable, providing a solid foundation as you build and scale your projects. In the next chapter, we'll wrap up with deployment strategies and tips for taking your PHP applications live.

Chapter 15: Deploying Your PHP Application

Once you've completed your PHP application, the final step is to deploy it to a live environment where users can access it. This chapter covers the essentials of preparing your PHP application for production, choosing the right hosting option, and implementing version control and continuous deployment workflows to streamline updates. With these deployment practices, you'll ensure a smooth, efficient, and secure transition from development to production.

Preparing for Production

Preparing your application for production involves optimizing, securing, and configuring it to handle real-world traffic and usage. Let's go through the essential steps.

1. Pre-Deployment Checklist

Before deploying, review the following checklist to ensure that your application is ready for production.

- **Error Reporting**: Disable error reporting to prevent users from seeing internal error messages that could expose sensitive information.

```php
php
```

```php
ini_set('display_errors', 0);

ini_set('log_errors', 1);
```

- **Environment Variables**: Use environment variables to store sensitive data, such as database credentials, API keys, and application settings. Tools like .env files and libraries like vlucas/phpdotenv make managing environment variables easy.

```php
php
```

```php
// Load environment variables

require 'vendor/autoload.php';

Dotenv\Dotenv::createImmutable(__DIR__)->load();
```

- **Database Configuration**: Optimize database queries, create necessary indexes, and remove test data. Back up the database before deploying.

- **Permissions**: Ensure correct file and folder permissions on the server to prevent unauthorized access. For example, restrict permissions on sensitive files like .env and set folders to read-only when possible.

- **Caching**: Enable caching to improve performance. Use an opcode cache like Opcache, and consider setting up data caching (e.g., Memcached or Redis) for frequently accessed information.

2. Enabling Error Logging

In production, disable error display and enable error logging. Set up error logs to capture and record issues without interrupting the user experience.

1. **Configure Error Logging**: Set up a centralized error log in your PHP configuration or php.ini file.

ini

log_errors = On

error_log = /var/log/php_errors.log

2. **Monitor Error Logs**: Regularly monitor your error logs or integrate logging services like Sentry, Papertrail, or Loggly to receive alerts about critical issues in real time.

3. **Graceful Error Handling**: Use custom error pages (like a 500 internal server error page) to display friendly error messages to users while logging technical details behind the scenes.

3. Optimizing for Production

Production optimization reduces load times and improves performance.

1. **Minify Assets**: Minify CSS, JavaScript, and HTML files to reduce file sizes. Tools like Gulp, Webpack, or online minifiers can automate this process.

2. **Enable GZIP Compression**: GZIP compresses server responses, reducing load times for users. Enable GZIP in your server configuration.

apache

```
# In .htaccess for Apache servers

AddOutputFilterByType DEFLATE text/html
text/plain text/xml text/css text/javascript
```

3. **Load Balancing and CDN**: If your application handles high traffic, consider using a Content Delivery Network (CDN) and load balancing to distribute the load and reduce latency.

Hosting Options

Choosing the right hosting environment is crucial for your application's performance, scalability, and cost-effectiveness. Let's explore different hosting options and their benefits.

1. Shared Hosting

Shared hosting is an affordable option where multiple websites share the same server resources. It's suitable for smaller projects or initial deployments with low traffic.

- **Pros**: Low cost, easy setup, basic technical support.
- **Cons**: Limited control over server configurations, slower performance under high load, limited scalability.

Recommended For: Small applications or early development stages where budget and simplicity are priorities.

2. Virtual Private Server (VPS)

A VPS provides a dedicated portion of a server, offering more resources and control than shared hosting. With a VPS, you have root access to configure the server as needed.

- **Pros**: Greater control, scalable resources, better performance than shared hosting.
- **Cons**: Requires server management skills, costs more than shared hosting.

Recommended For: Medium-sized applications with moderate traffic and the need for custom configurations.

3. Cloud Hosting

Cloud hosting providers like AWS, Google Cloud, and Azure offer flexible, scalable environments that automatically allocate resources based on demand. Many cloud services are pay-as-you-go, meaning you only pay for what you use.

- **Pros**: High scalability, global distribution, automated backups, and failover.

- **Cons**: Higher cost, complex setup and management, may require specialized skills.

Recommended For: Applications with high or unpredictable traffic and those requiring global reach or rapid scaling.

4. Dedicated Hosting

With dedicated hosting, you rent an entire server for your application, providing complete control and access to all resources.

- **Pros**: Full control, maximum performance, secure environment.

- **Cons**: Higher cost, requires server management skills, not easily scalable without additional hardware.

Recommended For: Large applications with high traffic and strict security or compliance requirements.

5. Platform-as-a-Service (PaaS)

PaaS providers like Heroku, DigitalOcean App Platform, and Laravel Forge offer a managed environment where you can deploy applications without handling server setup. These platforms take care of scaling, backups, and monitoring.

- **Pros**: Minimal setup, automatic scaling, managed environment.

- **Cons**: Limited customization, potentially higher cost for complex applications.

Recommended For: Developers who want to focus on the application rather than server management, or teams that need quick deployment with minimal setup.

Version Control and Continuous Deployment

Version control and continuous deployment streamline the process of updating and maintaining your application. Git is the most popular version control tool, and integrating it with automated workflows enables consistent and efficient deployments.

Using Git for Version Control

Git tracks code changes, allowing collaboration and version tracking. GitHub, GitLab, and Bitbucket are popular Git platforms with additional tools for project management and deployment.

Setting Up a Git Repository

1. **Initialize Git**: Initialize Git in your project directory.

bash

git init

2. **Commit Changes**: Add files to the repository and commit them.

bash

git add .

git commit -m "Initial commit"

3. **Push to Remote Repository**: Create a remote repository on GitHub, GitLab, or Bitbucket and push your code.

bash

git remote add origin https://github.com/username/repository.git

git push -u origin main

With Git, you can manage different branches, roll back changes, and work collaboratively on the codebase.

Setting Up Continuous Deployment (CD)

Continuous Deployment (CD) automates the process of deploying code changes, enabling rapid updates and reducing the risk of human error. Most CD workflows involve running tests, building the application, and deploying it automatically to the server if all checks pass.

Example: Setting Up CD with GitHub Actions

GitHub Actions is a powerful tool for automating CI/CD workflows. Here's how to set up a simple CD pipeline for a PHP application.

1. **Create a Workflow File**: In your repository, create a file named .github/workflows/deploy.yml.

2. **Define the Workflow Steps**: Add the following configuration to automate tests and deploy code to your server.

```yaml
name: Deploy Application

on:
  push:
```

```yaml
    branches:
      - main

  jobs:
    build:
      runs-on: ubuntu-latest

      steps:
        - name: Checkout Code
          uses: actions/checkout@v2

        - name: Set up PHP
          uses: shivammathur/setup-php@v2
          with:
            php-version: '8.0'

        - name: Install Dependencies
          run: composer install --no-dev --prefer-dist

        - name: Run Tests
          run: vendor/bin/phpunit
```

```yaml
deploy:
  runs-on: ubuntu-latest
  needs: build

  steps:
    - name: Deploy to Server
      env:
        SSH_KEY: ${{ secrets.SSH_KEY }}
      run: |
        ssh -i $SSH_KEY user@your-server.com "cd /path/to/project && git pull origin main && composer install --no-dev && php artisan migrate"
```

In this example:

- **On Push to Main Branch**: The workflow triggers when code is pushed to the main branch.

- **Install Dependencies and Run Tests**: Installs dependencies and runs unit tests to ensure the code is reliable.

- **Deploy to Server**: Deploys the code to the server by connecting via SSH, pulling changes, and running necessary commands like composer install.

3. **Setting Up SSH for Secure Deployment**: Use GitHub secrets to store an SSH key, allowing secure access to your server.

   o Generate an SSH key pair with ssh-keygen.

   o Add the public key to your server's authorized keys.

   o Add the private key to GitHub as a secret in your repository settings.

This GitHub Actions workflow automatically deploys changes whenever you push to the main branch, ensuring a streamlined and consistent deployment process.

Continuous Integration with Testing

Continuous Integration (CI) involves automatically running tests on every change. In the example above, Run Tests is part of the CI process, verifying code quality before deployment.

- **Automated Testing**: Use PHPUnit to run automated tests on each push, ensuring code changes don't introduce bugs.

- **Code Coverage Reports**: Generate reports on code coverage, identifying untested areas to improve test completeness.

Combining CI and CD ensures code quality and consistency, reducing manual effort and deployment risks.

Conclusion

Deploying a PHP application involves careful preparation, from optimizing for production to selecting a hosting environment and implementing automated deployment workflows. This chapter covered the pre-deployment checklist, including error logging, optimization, and configuration for production. We explored hosting options from shared hosting to cloud platforms, helping you choose the right fit for your application's needs and scale.

Finally, we looked at version control with Git and the power of continuous deployment workflows using GitHub Actions, which enable automatic testing, building, and deployment to ensure fast, reliable updates. By following these deployment practices, you'll be well-equipped to launch and maintain a secure, high-performance PHP application.